FORWARD/COMMENTARY

The National Institute of Standards and Technology (NIST) is a measurement standards laboratory, and a non-regulatory agency of the United States Department of Commerce. Its mission is to promote innovation and industrial competitiveness. Founded in 1901, as the National Bureau of Standards, NIST was formed with the mandate to provide standard weights and measures, and to serve as the national physical laboratory for the United States. With a world-class measurement and testing laboratory encompassing a wide range of areas of computer science, mathematics, statistics, and systems engineering, NIST's cybersecurity program supports its overall mission to promote U.S. innovation and industrial competitiveness by advancing measurement science, standards, and related technology through research and development in ways that enhance economic security and improve our quality of life.

The need for cybersecurity standards and best practices that address interoperability, usability and privacy has been shown to be critical for the nation. NIST's cybersecurity programs seek to enable greater development and application of practical, innovative security technologies and methodologies that enhance the country's ability to address current and future computer and information security challenges.

The cybersecurity publications produced by NIST cover a wide range of cybersecurity concepts that are carefully designed to work together to produce a holistic approach to cybersecurity primarily for government agencies and constitute the best practices used by industry. This holistic strategy to cybersecurity covers the gamut of security subjects from development of secure encryption standards for communication and storage of information while at rest to how best to recover from a cyber-attack.

Why buy a book you can download for free?

Some are available only in electronic media. Some online docs are missing pages or barely legible.

We at 4th Watch Books are former government employees, so we know how government employees actually use the standards. When a new standard is released, an engineer prints it out, punches holes and puts it in a 3-ring binder. While this is not a big deal for a 5 or 10-page document, many NIST documents are over 100 pages and printing a large document is a time-consuming effort. So, an engineer that's paid $75 an hour is spending hours simply printing out the tools needed to do the job. That's time that could be better spent doing engineering. We publish these documents so engineers can focus on what they were hired to do – engineering. It's much more cost-effective to just order the latest version from Amazon.com

If there is a standard you would like published, let us know. Our web site is Cybah.webplus.net

Please see the Cybersecurity Standards list at the end of this book.

CyberSecurity Standards Library™

NIST CNSS NERC CIP

Get a Complete Library of Over 300 Cybersecurity Standards on 1 Convenient DVD!

The **4th Watch CyberSecurity Standards Library** is a DVD disc that puts over 300 current and archived cybersecurity standards from NIST, DOD, DHS, CNSS and NERC at your fingertips! Many of these cybersecurity standards are hard to find and we included the current version and a previous version for many of them. The DVD includes four books written by Luis Ayala: **The Cyber Dictionary, Cybersecurity Standards**, **Cyber-Security Glossary of Building Hacks and Cyber-Attacks**, and **Cyber-Physical Attack Defenses: Preventing Damage to Buildings and Utilities**.

- ✓ DVD includes many Hard-to-find Cybersecurity Standards - some still in Draft.
- ✓ Docs are organized by source and listed numerically so each standard is easy to locate.
- ✓ The listing of standards on the DVD includes an abstract of the subject, and date issued.
- ✓ PDF format for use on PC, Mac, eReaders, or tablets.
- ✓ No need for WiFi / Internet.
- ✓ Save countless hours of searching and downloading.
- ✓ Carry in a briefcase - terrific for travel.

4th Watch Publishing is releasing the CyberSecurity Standards Library DVD to make it easier for you to access the tools you need to ensure the security of your computer networks and SCADA systems. We also publish many of these standards on demand so you don't need to waste valuable time searching for the latest version of a standard, printing hundreds of pages and punching holes so they can go in a three-ring binder. **Order on Amazon.com**

The DVD works on PC and Mac with the standards in PDF format. To view the CyberSecurity Standards Library on the DVD, a computer with a DVD drive is required. The most current version of your internet browser, at least 2GB of RAM, and current version of Adobe Reader is recommended. (Compatible browsers include Internet Explorer 8+, Mozilla Firefox 4+, Apple Safari 5+, Google Chrome 15+)

Federal Information

Processing Standards Publication 197

November 26, 2001

Announcing the

ADVANCED ENCRYPTION STANDARD (AES)

Federal Information Processing Standards Publications (FIPS PUBS) are issued by the National Institute of Standards and Technology (NIST) after approval by the Secretary of Commerce pursuant to Section 5131 of the Information Technology Management Reform Act of 1996 (Public Law 104-106) and the Computer Security Act of 1987 (Public Law 100-235).

1. **Name of Standard.** Advanced Encryption Standard (AES) (FIPS PUB 197).

2. **Category of Standard.** Computer Security Standard, Cryptography.

3. **Explanation.** The Advanced Encryption Standard (AES) specifies a FIPS-approved cryptographic algorithm that can be used to protect electronic data. The AES algorithm is a symmetric block cipher that can encrypt (encipher) and decrypt (decipher) information. Encryption converts data to an unintelligible form called ciphertext; decrypting the ciphertext converts the data back into its original form, called plaintext.

The AES algorithm is capable of using cryptographic keys of 128, 192, and 256 bits to encrypt and decrypt data in blocks of 128 bits.

4. **Approving Authority.** Secretary of Commerce.

5. **Maintenance Agency.** Department of Commerce, National Institute of Standards and Technology, Information Technology Laboratory (ITL).

6. **Applicability.** This standard may be used by Federal departments and agencies when an agency determines that sensitive (unclassified) information (as defined in P. L. 100-235) requires cryptographic protection.

Other FIPS-approved cryptographic algorithms may be used in addition to, or in lieu of, this standard. Federal agencies or departments that use cryptographic devices for protecting classified information can use those devices for protecting sensitive (unclassified) information in lieu of this standard.

In addition, this standard may be adopted and used by non-Federal Government organizations. Such use is encouraged when it provides the desired security for commercial and private organizations.

7. Specifications. Federal Information Processing Standard (FIPS) 197, Advanced Encryption Standard (AES) (affixed).

8. Implementations. The algorithm specified in this standard may be implemented in software, firmware, hardware, or any combination thereof. The specific implementation may depend on several factors such as the application, the environment, the technology used, etc. The algorithm shall be used in conjunction with a FIPS approved or NIST recommended mode of operation. Object Identifiers (OIDs) and any associated parameters for AES used in these modes are available at the Computer Security Objects Register (CSOR), located at http://csrc.nist.gov/csor/ [2].

Implementations of the algorithm that are tested by an accredited laboratory and validated will be considered as complying with this standard. Since cryptographic security depends on many factors besides the correct implementation of an encryption algorithm, Federal Government employees, and others, should also refer to NIST Special Publication 800-21, *Guideline for Implementing Cryptography in the Federal Government*, for additional information and guidance (NIST SP 800-21 is available at http://csrc.nist.gov/publications/).

9. Implementation Schedule. This standard becomes effective on May 26, 2002.

10. Patents. Implementations of the algorithm specified in this standard may be covered by U.S. and foreign patents.

11. Export Control. Certain cryptographic devices and technical data regarding them are subject to Federal export controls. Exports of cryptographic modules implementing this standard and technical data regarding them must comply with these Federal regulations and be licensed by the Bureau of Export Administration of the U.S. Department of Commerce. Applicable Federal government export controls are specified in Title 15, Code of Federal Regulations (CFR) Part 740.17; Title 15, CFR Part 742; and Title 15, CFR Part 774, Category 5, Part 2.

12. Qualifications. NIST will continue to follow developments in the analysis of the AES algorithm. As with its other cryptographic algorithm standards, NIST will formally reevaluate this standard every five years.

Both this standard and possible threats reducing the security provided through the use of this standard will undergo review by NIST as appropriate, taking into account newly available analysis and technology. In addition, the awareness of any breakthrough in technology or any mathematical weakness of the algorithm will cause NIST to reevaluate this standard and provide necessary revisions.

13. Waiver Procedure. Under certain exceptional circumstances, the heads of Federal agencies, or their delegates, may approve waivers to Federal Information Processing Standards (FIPS). The heads of such agencies may redelegate such authority only to a senior official designated pursuant to Section 3506(b) of Title 44, U.S. Code. Waivers shall be granted only when compliance with this standard would

a. adversely affect the accomplishment of the mission of an operator of Federal computer system or

b. cause a major adverse financial impact on the operator that is not offset by government-wide savings.

Agency heads may act upon a written waiver request containing the information detailed above. Agency heads may also act without a written waiver request when they determine that conditions for meeting the standard cannot be met. Agency heads may approve waivers only by a written decision that explains the basis on which the agency head made the required finding(s). A copy of each such decision, with procurement sensitive or classified portions clearly identified, shall be sent to: National Institute of Standards and Technology; ATTN: FIPS Waiver Decision, Information Technology Laboratory, 100 Bureau Drive, Stop 8900, Gaithersburg, MD 20899-8900.

In addition, notice of each waiver granted and each delegation of authority to approve waivers shall be sent promptly to the Committee on Government Operations of the House of Representatives and the Committee on Government Affairs of the Senate and shall be published promptly in the Federal Register.

When the determination on a waiver applies to the procurement of equipment and/or services, a notice of the waiver determination must be published in the Commerce Business Daily as a part of the notice of solicitation for offers of an acquisition or, if the waiver determination is made after that notice is published, by amendment to such notice.

A copy of the waiver, any supporting documents, the document approving the waiver and any supporting and accompanying documents, with such deletions as the agency is authorized and decides to make under Section 552(b) of Title 5, U.S. Code, shall be part of the procurement documentation and retained by the agency.

14. Where to obtain copies. This publication is available electronically by accessing http://csrc.nist.gov/publications/. A list of other available computer security publications, including ordering information, can be obtained from NIST Publications List 91, which is available at the same web site. Alternatively, copies of NIST computer security publications are available from: National Technical Information Service (NTIS), 5285 Port Royal Road, Springfield, VA 22161.

Federal Information

Processing Standards Publication 197

November 26, 2001

Specification for the

ADVANCED ENCRYPTION STANDARD (AES)

Table of Contents

Table of Figures

1. Introduction

This standard specifies the **Rijndael** algorithm ([3] and [4]), a symmetric block cipher that can process **data blocks** of **128 bits**, using cipher **keys** with lengths of **128**, **192**, and **256 bits**. Rijndael was designed to handle additional block sizes and key lengths, however they are not adopted in this standard.

Throughout the remainder of this standard, the algorithm specified herein will be referred to as "the AES algorithm." The algorithm may be used with the three different key lengths indicated above, and therefore these different "flavors" may be referred to as "AES-128", "AES-192", and "AES-256".

This specification includes the following sections:

2. Definitions of terms, acronyms, and algorithm parameters, symbols, and functions;
3. Notation and conventions used in the algorithm specification, including the ordering and numbering of bits, bytes, and words;
4. Mathematical properties that are useful in understanding the algorithm;
5. Algorithm specification, covering the key expansion, encryption, and decryption routines;
6. Implementation issues, such as key length support, keying restrictions, and additional block/key/round sizes.

The standard concludes with several appendices that include step-by-step examples for Key Expansion and the Cipher, example vectors for the Cipher and Inverse Cipher, and a list of references.

2. Definitions

2.1 Glossary of Terms and Acronyms

The following definitions are used throughout this standard:

AES	Advanced Encryption Standard
Affine Transformation	A transformation consisting of multiplication by a matrix followed by the addition of a vector.
Array	An enumerated collection of identical entities (e.g., an array of bytes).
Bit	A binary digit having a value of 0 or 1.
Block	Sequence of binary bits that comprise the input, output, State, and Round Key. The length of a sequence is the number of bits it contains. Blocks are also interpreted as arrays of bytes.
Byte	A group of eight bits that is treated either as a single entity or as an array of 8 individual bits.

Cipher	Series of transformations that converts plaintext to ciphertext using the Cipher Key.
Cipher Key	Secret, cryptographic key that is used by the Key Expansion routine to generate a set of Round Keys; can be pictured as a rectangular array of bytes, having four rows and ***Nk*** columns.
Ciphertext	Data output from the Cipher or input to the Inverse Cipher.
Inverse Cipher	Series of transformations that converts ciphertext to plaintext using the Cipher Key.
Key Expansion	Routine used to generate a series of Round Keys from the Cipher Key.
Plaintext	Data input to the Cipher or output from the Inverse Cipher.
Rijndael	Cryptographic algorithm specified in this Advanced Encryption Standard (AES).
Round Key	Round keys are values derived from the Cipher Key using the Key Expansion routine; they are applied to the State in the Cipher and Inverse Cipher.
State	Intermediate Cipher result that can be pictured as a rectangular array of bytes, having four rows and ***Nb*** columns.
S-box	Non-linear substitution table used in several byte substitution transformations and in the Key Expansion routine to perform a one-for-one substitution of a byte value.
Word	A group of 32 bits that is treated either as a single entity or as an array of 4 bytes.

2.2 Algorithm Parameters, Symbols, and Functions

The following algorithm parameters, symbols, and functions are used throughout this standard:

`AddRoundKey()`	Transformation in the Cipher and Inverse Cipher in which a Round Key is added to the State using an XOR operation. The length of a Round Key equals the size of the State (i.e., for *Nb* = 4, the Round Key length equals 128 bits/16 bytes).
`InvMixColumns()`	Transformation in the Inverse Cipher that is the inverse of **`MixColumns()`**.
`InvShiftRows()`	Transformation in the Inverse Cipher that is the inverse of **`ShiftRows()`**.
`InvSubBytes()`	Transformation in the Inverse Cipher that is the inverse of **`SubBytes()`**.
K	Cipher Key.

`MixColumns()`	Transformation in the Cipher that takes all of the columns of the State and mixes their data (independently of one another) to produce new columns.
Nb	Number of columns (32-bit words) comprising the State. For this standard, ***Nb*** = 4. (Also see Sec. 6.3.)
Nk	Number of 32-bit words comprising the Cipher Key. For this standard, ***Nk*** = 4, 6, or 8. (Also see Sec. 6.3.)
Nr	Number of rounds, which is a function of ***Nk*** and ***Nb*** (which is fixed). For this standard, ***Nr*** = 10, 12, or 14. (Also see Sec. 6.3.)
Rcon[]	The round constant word array.
`RotWord()`	Function used in the Key Expansion routine that takes a four-byte word and performs a cyclic permutation.
`ShiftRows()`	Transformation in the Cipher that processes the State by cyclically shifting the last three rows of the State by different offsets.
`SubBytes()`	Transformation in the Cipher that processes the State using a non-linear byte substitution table (S-box) that operates on each of the State bytes independently.
`SubWord()`	Function used in the Key Expansion routine that takes a four-byte input word and applies an S-box to each of the four bytes to produce an output word.
XOR	Exclusive-OR operation.
$\oplus$	Exclusive-OR operation.
$\otimes$	Multiplication of two polynomials (each with degree < 4) modulo $x^4 + 1$.
$\bullet$	Finite field multiplication.

3. Notation and Conventions

3.1 Inputs and Outputs

The **input** and **output** for the AES algorithm each consist of **sequences of 128 bits** (digits with values of 0 or 1). These sequences will sometimes be referred to as **blocks** and the number of bits they contain will be referred to as their length. The **Cipher Key** for the AES algorithm is a **sequence of 128, 192 or 256 bits**. Other input, output and Cipher Key lengths are not permitted by this standard.

The bits within such sequences will be numbered starting at zero and ending at one less than the sequence length (block length or key length). The number i attached to a bit is known as its index and will be in one of the ranges $0 \le i < 128$, $0 \le i < 192$ or $0 \le i < 256$ depending on the block length and key length (specified above).

3.2 Bytes

The basic unit for processing in the AES algorithm is a **byte,** a sequence of eight bits treated as a single entity. The input, output and Cipher Key bit sequences described in Sec. 3.1 are processed as arrays of bytes that are formed by dividing these sequences into groups of eight contiguous bits to form arrays of bytes (see Sec. 3.3). For an input, output or Cipher Key denoted by a, the bytes in the resulting array will be referenced using one of the two forms, a_n or $a[n]$, where n will be in one of the following ranges:

Key length = 128 bits, $0 \le n < 16$; Block length = 128 bits, $0 \le n < 16$;

Key length = 192 bits, $0 \le n < 24$;

Key length = 256 bits, $0 \le n < 32$.

All byte values in the AES algorithm will be presented as the concatenation of its individual bit values (0 or 1) between braces in the order $\{b_7, b_6, b_5, b_4, b_3, b_2, b_1, b_0\}$. These bytes are interpreted as finite field elements using a polynomial representation:

$$b_7x^7 + b_6x^6 + b_5x^5 + b_4x^4 + b_3x^3 + b_2x^2 + b_1x + b_0 = \sum_{i=0}^{7} b_i x^i . \qquad (3.1)$$

For example, {01100011} identifies the specific finite field element $x^6 + x^5 + x + 1$.

It is also convenient to denote byte values using hexadecimal notation with each of two groups of four bits being denoted by a single character as in Fig. 1.

Bit Pattern	Character	Bit Pattern	Character	Bit Pattern	Character	Bit Pattern	Character
0000	0	0100	4	1000	8	1100	c
0001	1	0101	5	1001	9	1101	d
0010	2	0110	6	1010	a	1110	e
0011	3	0111	7	1011	b	1111	f

Figure 1. Hexadecimal representation of bit patterns.

Hence the element {01100011} can be represented as {63}, where the character denoting the four-bit group containing the higher numbered bits is again to the left.

Some finite field operations involve one additional bit (b_8) to the left of an 8-bit byte. Where this extra bit is present, it will appear as '{01}' immediately preceding the 8-bit byte; for example, a 9-bit sequence will be presented as {01}{1b}.

3.3 Arrays of Bytes

Arrays of bytes will be represented in the following form:

$$a_0 a_1 a_2 \ldots a_{15}$$

The bytes and the bit ordering within bytes are derived from the 128-bit input sequence

$$input_0\ input_1\ input_2\ \ldots\ input_{126}\ input_{127}$$

as follows:

$$a_0 = \{input_0, input_1, \ldots, input_7\};$$

$$a_1 = \{input_8, input_9, \ldots, input_{15}\};$$

$$\vdots$$

$$a_{15} = \{input_{120}, input_{121}, \ldots, input_{127}\}.$$

The pattern can be extended to longer sequences (i.e., for 192- and 256-bit keys), so that, in general,

$$a_n = \{input_{8n}, input_{8n+1}, \ldots, input_{8n+7}\}. \qquad (3.2)$$

Taking Sections 3.2 and 3.3 together, Fig. 2 shows how bits within each byte are numbered.

Input bit sequence	0	1	2	3	4	5	6	7	8	9	10	11	12	13	14	15	16	17	18	19	20	21	22	23	…
Byte number	0								1								2								…
Bit numbers in byte	7	6	5	4	3	2	1	0	7	6	5	4	3	2	1	0	7	6	5	4	3	2	1	0	…

Figure 2. Indices for Bytes and Bits.

3.4 The State

Internally, the AES algorithm's operations are performed on a two-dimensional array of bytes called the **State**. The State consists of four rows of bytes, each containing ***Nb*** bytes, where ***Nb*** is the block length divided by 32. In the State array denoted by the symbol s, each individual byte has two indices, with its row number r in the range $0 \le r < 4$ and its column number c in the range $0 \le c < \boldsymbol{Nb}$. This allows an individual byte of the State to be referred to as either $s_{r,c}$ or $s[r,c]$. For this standard, ***Nb***=4, i.e., $0 \le c < 4$ (also see Sec. 6.3).

At the start of the Cipher and Inverse Cipher described in Sec. 5, the input – the array of bytes in_0, in_1, … in_{15} – is copied into the State array as illustrated in Fig. 3. The Cipher or Inverse Cipher operations are then conducted on this State array, after which its final value is copied to the output – the array of bytes out_0, out_1, … out_{15}.

input bytes

in_0	in_4	in_8	in_{12}
in_1	in_5	in_9	in_{13}
in_2	in_6	in_{10}	in_{14}
in_3	in_7	in_{11}	in_{15}

→

State array

$s_{0,0}$	$s_{0,1}$	$s_{0,2}$	$s_{0,3}$
$s_{1,0}$	$s_{1,1}$	$s_{1,2}$	$s_{1,3}$
$s_{2,0}$	$s_{2,1}$	$s_{2,2}$	$s_{2,3}$
$s_{3,0}$	$s_{3,1}$	$s_{3,2}$	$s_{3,3}$

→

output bytes

out_0	out_4	out_8	out_{12}
out_1	out_5	out_9	out_{13}
out_2	out_6	out_{10}	out_{14}
out_3	out_7	out_{11}	out_{15}

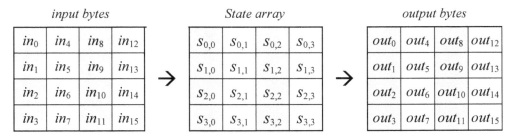

Figure 3. State array input and output.

Hence, at the beginning of the Cipher or Inverse Cipher, the input array, *in*, is copied to the State array according to the scheme:

$$s[r, c] = in[r + 4c] \qquad \text{for } 0 \le r < 4 \text{ and } 0 \le c < Nb, \qquad (3.3)$$

and at the end of the Cipher and Inverse Cipher, the State is copied to the output array *out* as follows:

$$out[r + 4c] = s[r, c] \qquad \text{for } 0 \le r < 4 \text{ and } 0 \le c < Nb. \qquad (3.4)$$

3.5 The State as an Array of Columns

The four bytes in each column of the State array form 32-bit **words**, where the row number r provides an index for the four bytes within each word. The state can hence be interpreted as a one-dimensional array of 32 bit words (columns), $w_0...w_3$, where the column number c provides an index into this array. Hence, for the example in Fig. 3, the State can be considered as an array of four words, as follows:

$$w_0 = s_{0,0}\ s_{1,0}\ s_{2,0}\ s_{3,0} \qquad w_2 = s_{0,2}\ s_{1,2}\ s_{2,2}\ s_{3,2}$$

$$w_1 = s_{0,1}\ s_{1,1}\ s_{2,1}\ s_{3,1} \qquad w_3 = s_{0,3}\ s_{1,3}\ s_{2,3}\ s_{3,3}\ . \qquad (3.5)$$

4. Mathematical Preliminaries

All bytes in the AES algorithm are interpreted as finite field elements using the notation introduced in Sec. 3.2. Finite field elements can be added and multiplied, but these operations are different from those used for numbers. The following subsections introduce the basic mathematical concepts needed for Sec. 5.

4.1 Addition

The addition of two elements in a finite field is achieved by "adding" the coefficients for the corresponding powers in the polynomials for the two elements. The addition is performed with the XOR operation (denoted by $\oplus$) - i.e., modulo 2 - so that $1 \oplus 1 = 0$, $1 \oplus 0 = 1$, and $0 \oplus 0 = 0$. Consequently, subtraction of polynomials is identical to addition of polynomials.

Alternatively, addition of finite field elements can be described as the modulo 2 addition of corresponding bits in the byte. For two bytes $\{a_7a_6a_5a_4a_3a_2a_1a_0\}$ and $\{b_7b_6b_5b_4b_3b_2b_1b_0\}$, the sum is $\{c_7c_6c_5c_4c_3c_2c_1c_0\}$, where each $c_i = a_i \oplus b_i$ (i.e., $c_7 = a_7 \oplus b_7$, $c_6 = a_6 \oplus b_6$, $...c_0 = a_0 \oplus b_0$).

For example, the following expressions are equivalent to one another:

$$(x^6 + x^4 + x^2 + x + 1) + (x^7 + x + 1) = x^7 + x^6 + x^4 + x^2 \qquad \text{(polynomial notation);}$$

$$\{01010111\} \oplus \{10000011\} = \{11010100\} \qquad \text{(binary notation);}$$

$$\{57\} \oplus \{83\} = \{d4\} \qquad \text{(hexadecimal notation).}$$

4.2 Multiplication

In the polynomial representation, multiplication in $GF(2^8)$ (denoted by $\bullet$) corresponds with the multiplication of polynomials modulo an **irreducible polynomial** of degree 8. A polynomial is irreducible if its only divisors are one and itself. **For the AES algorithm, this irreducible polynomial is**

$$m(x) = x^8 + x^4 + x^3 + x + 1, \qquad (4.1)$$

or {01}{1b} in hexadecimal notation.

For example, {57} • {83} = {c1}, because

$$
\begin{aligned}
(x^6 + x^4 + x^2 + x + 1)\,(x^7 + x + 1) &= x^{13} + x^{11} + x^9 + x^8 + x^7 + \\
&\quad x^7 + x^5 + x^3 + x^2 + x + \\
&\quad x^6 + x^4 + x^2 + x + 1 \\
&= x^{13} + x^{11} + x^9 + x^8 + x^6 + x^5 + x^4 + x^3 + 1
\end{aligned}
$$

and

$$
\begin{aligned}
x^{13} + x^{11} + x^9 + x^8 + x^6 + x^5 + x^4 + x^3 + 1 \ \texttt{modulo}\ (x^8 + x^4 + x^3 + x + 1) \\
= x^7 + x^6 + 1.
\end{aligned}
$$

The modular reduction by $m(x)$ ensures that the result will be a binary polynomial of degree less than 8, and thus can be represented by a byte. Unlike addition, there is no simple operation at the byte level that corresponds to this multiplication.

The multiplication defined above is associative, and the element {01} is the multiplicative identity. For any non-zero binary polynomial $b(x)$ of degree less than 8, the multiplicative inverse of $b(x)$, denoted $b^{-1}(x)$, can be found as follows: the extended Euclidean algorithm [7] is used to compute polynomials $a(x)$ and $c(x)$ such that

$$b(x)a(x) + m(x)c(x) = 1. \tag{4.2}$$

Hence, $a(x) \bullet b(x) \bmod m(x) = 1$, which means

$$b^{-1}(x) = a(x) \bmod m(x). \tag{4.3}$$

Moreover, for any $a(x)$, $b(x)$ and $c(x)$ in the field, it holds that

$$a(x) \bullet (b(x) + c(x)) = a(x) \bullet b(x) + a(x) \bullet c(x).$$

It follows that the set of 256 possible byte values, with XOR used as addition and the multiplication defined as above, has the structure of the finite field GF(2^8).

4.2.1 Multiplication by x

Multiplying the binary polynomial defined in equation (3.1) with the polynomial x results in

$$b_7x^8 + b_6x^7 + b_5x^6 + b_4x^5 + b_3x^4 + b_2x^3 + b_1x^2 + b_0x. \tag{4.4}$$

The result $x \bullet b(x)$ is obtained by reducing the above result modulo $m(x)$, as defined in equation (4.1). If $b_7 = 0$, the result is already in reduced form. If $b_7 = 1$, the reduction is accomplished by subtracting (i.e., XORing) the polynomial $m(x)$. It follows that multiplication by x (i.e., {00000010} or {02}) can be implemented at the byte level as a left shift and a subsequent conditional bitwise XOR with {1b}. This operation on bytes is denoted by `xtime()`. Multiplication by higher powers of x can be implemented by repeated application of `xtime()`. By adding intermediate results, multiplication by any constant can be implemented.

For example, {57} • {13} = {fe} because

$$\begin{aligned}\{57\} \bullet \{02\} &= \mathtt{xtime}(\{57\}) = \{ae\} \\ \{57\} \bullet \{04\} &= \mathtt{xtime}(\{ae\}) = \{47\} \\ \{57\} \bullet \{08\} &= \mathtt{xtime}(\{47\}) = \{8e\} \\ \{57\} \bullet \{10\} &= \mathtt{xtime}(\{8e\}) = \{07\},\end{aligned}$$

thus,

$$\begin{aligned}\{57\} \bullet \{13\} &= \{57\} \bullet (\{01\} \oplus \{02\} \oplus \{10\}) \\ &= \{57\} \oplus \{ae\} \oplus \{07\} \\ &= \{fe\}.\end{aligned}$$

4.3 Polynomials with Coefficients in GF(2^8)

Four-term polynomials can be defined - with coefficients that are finite field elements - as:

$$a(x) = a_3x^3 + a_2x^2 + a_1x + a_0 \tag{4.5}$$

which will be denoted as a word in the form $[a_0, a_1, a_2, a_3]$. Note that the polynomials in this section behave somewhat differently than the polynomials used in the definition of finite field elements, even though both types of polynomials use the same indeterminate, x. The coefficients in this section are themselves finite field elements, i.e., bytes, instead of bits; also, the multiplication of four-term polynomials uses a different reduction polynomial, defined below. The distinction should always be clear from the context.

To illustrate the addition and multiplication operations, let

$$b(x) = b_3x^3 + b_2x^2 + b_1x + b_0 \tag{4.6}$$

define a second four-term polynomial. Addition is performed by adding the finite field coefficients of like powers of x. This addition corresponds to an XOR operation between the corresponding bytes in each of the words – in other words, the XOR of the complete word values.

Thus, using the equations of (4.5) and (4.6),

$$a(x) + b(x) = (a_3 \oplus b_3)x^3 + (a_2 \oplus b_2)x^2 + (a_1 \oplus b_1)x + (a_0 \oplus b_0) \tag{4.7}$$

Multiplication is achieved in two steps. In the first step, the polynomial product $c(x) = a(x) \bullet b(x)$ is algebraically expanded, and like powers are collected to give

$$c(x) = c_6x^6 + c_5x^5 + c_4x^4 + c_3x^3 + c_2x^2 + c_1x + c_0 \tag{4.8}$$

where

$$\begin{aligned}c_0 &= a_0 \bullet b_0 & c_4 &= a_3 \bullet b_1 \oplus a_2 \bullet b_2 \oplus a_1 \bullet b_3 \\ c_1 &= a_1 \bullet b_0 \oplus a_0 \bullet b_1 & c_5 &= a_3 \bullet b_2 \oplus a_2 \bullet b_3 \\ c_2 &= a_2 \bullet b_0 \oplus a_1 \bullet b_1 \oplus a_0 \bullet b_2 & c_6 &= a_3 \bullet b_3\end{aligned} \tag{4.9}$$

$$c_3 = a_3 \bullet b_0 \oplus a_2 \bullet b_1 \oplus a_1 \bullet b_2 \oplus a_0 \bullet b_3 .$$

The result, $c(x)$, does not represent a four-byte word. Therefore, the second step of the multiplication is to reduce $c(x)$ modulo a polynomial of degree 4; the result can be reduced to a polynomial of degree less than 4. **For the AES algorithm, this is accomplished with the polynomial $x^4 + 1$**, so that

$$x^i \bmod(x^4 + 1) = x^{i \bmod 4} . \qquad (4.10)$$

The modular product of $a(x)$ and $b(x)$, denoted by $a(x) \otimes b(x)$, is given by the four-term polynomial $d(x)$, defined as follows:

$$d(x) = d_3 x^3 + d_2 x^2 + d_1 x + d_0 \qquad (4.11)$$

with

$$\begin{aligned} d_0 &= (a_0 \bullet b_0) \oplus (a_3 \bullet b_1) \oplus (a_2 \bullet b_2) \oplus (a_1 \bullet b_3) \\ d_1 &= (a_1 \bullet b_0) \oplus (a_0 \bullet b_1) \oplus (a_3 \bullet b_2) \oplus (a_2 \bullet b_3) \\ d_2 &= (a_2 \bullet b_0) \oplus (a_1 \bullet b_1) \oplus (a_0 \bullet b_2) \oplus (a_3 \bullet b_3) \\ d_3 &= (a_3 \bullet b_0) \oplus (a_2 \bullet b_1) \oplus (a_1 \bullet b_2) \oplus (a_0 \bullet b_3) \end{aligned} \qquad (4.12)$$

When $a(x)$ is a fixed polynomial, the operation defined in equation (4.11) can be written in matrix form as:

$$\begin{bmatrix} d_0 \\ d_1 \\ d_2 \\ d_3 \end{bmatrix} = \begin{bmatrix} a_0 & a_3 & a_2 & a_1 \\ a_1 & a_0 & a_3 & a_2 \\ a_2 & a_1 & a_0 & a_3 \\ a_3 & a_2 & a_1 & a_0 \end{bmatrix} \begin{bmatrix} b_0 \\ b_1 \\ b_2 \\ b_3 \end{bmatrix} \qquad (4.13)$$

Because $x^4 + 1$ is not an irreducible polynomial over $GF(2^8)$, multiplication by a fixed four-term polynomial is not necessarily invertible. However, the AES algorithm specifies a fixed four-term polynomial that *does* have an inverse (see Sec. 5.1.3 and Sec. 5.3.3):

$$a(x) = \{03\}x^3 + \{01\}x^2 + \{01\}x + \{02\} \qquad (4.14)$$

$$a^{-1}(x) = \{0b\}x^3 + \{0d\}x^2 + \{09\}x + \{0e\}. \qquad (4.15)$$

Another polynomial used in the AES algorithm (see the **`RotWord()`** function in Sec. 5.2) has $a_0 = a_1 = a_2 = \{00\}$ and $a_3 = \{01\}$, which is the polynomial x^3. Inspection of equation (4.13) above will show that its effect is to form the output word by rotating bytes in the input word. This means that $[b_0, b_1, b_2, b_3]$ is transformed into $[b_1, b_2, b_3, b_0]$.

5. Algorithm Specification

For the AES algorithm, **the length of the input block, the output block and the State is 128 bits.** This is represented by ***Nb*** = 4, which reflects the number of 32-bit words (number of columns) in the State.

For the AES algorithm**, the length of the Cipher Key, *K*, is 128, 192, or 256 bits.** The key length is represented by ***Nk*** = 4, 6, or 8, which reflects the number of 32-bit words (number of columns) in the Cipher Key.

For the AES algorithm, the number of rounds to be performed during the execution of the algorithm is dependent on the key size. The number of rounds is represented by ***Nr***, where ***Nr*** = 10 when ***Nk*** = 4, ***Nr*** = 12 when ***Nk*** = 6, and ***Nr*** = 14 when ***Nk*** = 8.

The only Key-Block-Round combinations that conform to this standard are given in Fig. 4. For implementation issues relating to the key length, block size and number of rounds, see Sec. 6.3.

	Key Length (*Nk words*)	Block Size (*Nb words*)	Number of Rounds (*Nr*)
AES-128	4	4	10
AES-192	6	4	12
AES-256	8	4	14

Figure 4. Key-Block-Round Combinations.

For both its Cipher and Inverse Cipher, the AES algorithm uses a round function that is composed of four different byte-oriented transformations: 1) byte substitution using a substitution table (S-box), 2) shifting rows of the State array by different offsets, 3) mixing the data within each column of the State array, and 4) adding a Round Key to the State. These transformations (and their inverses) are described in Sec. 5.1.1-5.1.4 and 5.3.1-5.3.4.

The Cipher and Inverse Cipher are described in Sec. 5.1 and Sec. 5.3, respectively, while the Key Schedule is described in Sec. 5.2.

5.1 Cipher

At the start of the Cipher, the input is copied to the State array using the conventions described in Sec. 3.4. After an initial Round Key addition, the State array is transformed by implementing a round function 10, 12, or 14 times (depending on the key length), with the final round differing slightly from the first ***Nr*** −1 rounds. The final State is then copied to the output as described in Sec. 3.4.

The round function is parameterized using a key schedule that consists of a one-dimensional array of four-byte words derived using the Key Expansion routine described in Sec. 5.2.

The Cipher is described in the pseudo code in Fig. 5. The individual transformations - **`SubBytes()`**, **`ShiftRows()`**, **`MixColumns()`**, and **`AddRoundKey()`** – process the State and are described in the following subsections. In Fig. 5, the array **`w[]`** contains the key schedule, which is described in Sec. 5.2.

As shown in Fig. 5, all ***Nr*** rounds are identical with the exception of the final round, which does not include the **`MixColumns()`** transformation.

Appendix B presents an example of the Cipher, showing values for the State array at the beginning of each round and after the application of each of the four transformations described in the following sections.

```
Cipher(byte in[4*Nb], byte out[4*Nb], word w[Nb*(Nr+1)])
begin
   byte  state[4,Nb]

   state = in

   AddRoundKey(state, w[0, Nb-1])              // See Sec. 5.1.4

   for round = 1 step 1 to Nr-1
      SubBytes(state)                          // See Sec. 5.1.1
      ShiftRows(state)                         // See Sec. 5.1.2
      MixColumns(state)                        // See Sec. 5.1.3
      AddRoundKey(state, w[round*Nb, (round+1)*Nb-1])
   end for

   SubBytes(state)
   ShiftRows(state)
   AddRoundKey(state, w[Nr*Nb, (Nr+1)*Nb-1])

   out = state
end
```

Figure 5. Pseudo Code for the Cipher.[1]

5.1.1 `SubBytes()` Transformation

The **`SubBytes()`** transformation is a non-linear byte substitution that operates independently on each byte of the State using a substitution table (S-box). This S-box (Fig. 7), which is invertible, is constructed by composing two transformations:

1. Take the multiplicative inverse in the finite field GF(2^8), described in Sec. 4.2; the element {`00`} is mapped to itself.
2. Apply the following affine transformation (over GF(2)):

$$b_i' = b_i \oplus b_{(i+4)\bmod 8} \oplus b_{(i+5)\bmod 8} \oplus b_{(i+6)\bmod 8} \oplus b_{(i+7)\bmod 8} \oplus c_i \qquad (5.1)$$

   for $0 \le i < 8$, where b_i is the ith bit of the byte, and c_i is the ith bit of a byte c with the value {`63`} or {`01100011`}. Here and elsewhere, a prime on a variable (e.g., b') indicates that the variable is to be updated with the value on the right.

   In matrix form, the affine transformation element of the S-box can be expressed as:

---

[1] The various transformations (e.g., **`SubBytes()`**, **`ShiftRows()`**, etc.) act upon the State array that is addressed by the '`state`' pointer. **`AddRoundKey()`** uses an additional pointer to address the Round Key.

$$\begin{bmatrix} b_0' \\ b_1' \\ b_2' \\ b_3' \\ b_4' \\ b_5' \\ b_6' \\ b_7' \end{bmatrix} = \begin{bmatrix} 1 & 0 & 0 & 0 & 1 & 1 & 1 & 1 \\ 1 & 1 & 0 & 0 & 0 & 1 & 1 & 1 \\ 1 & 1 & 1 & 0 & 0 & 0 & 1 & 1 \\ 1 & 1 & 1 & 1 & 0 & 0 & 0 & 1 \\ 1 & 1 & 1 & 1 & 1 & 0 & 0 & 0 \\ 0 & 1 & 1 & 1 & 1 & 1 & 0 & 0 \\ 0 & 0 & 1 & 1 & 1 & 1 & 1 & 0 \\ 0 & 0 & 0 & 1 & 1 & 1 & 1 & 1 \end{bmatrix} \begin{bmatrix} b_0 \\ b_1 \\ b_2 \\ b_3 \\ b_4 \\ b_5 \\ b_6 \\ b_7 \end{bmatrix} + \begin{bmatrix} 1 \\ 1 \\ 0 \\ 0 \\ 0 \\ 1 \\ 1 \\ 0 \end{bmatrix} . \tag{5.2}$$

Figure 6 illustrates the effect of the **`SubBytes()`** transformation on the State.

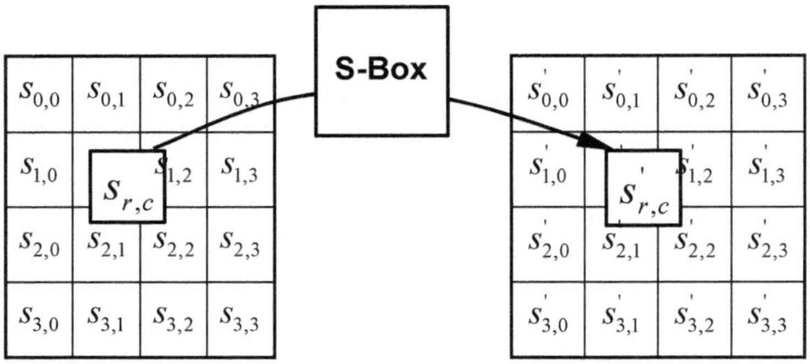

Figure 6. `SubBytes()` applies the S-box to each byte of the State.

The S-box used in the **`SubBytes()`** transformation is presented in hexadecimal form in Fig. 7. For example, if $s_{1,1} = \{53\}$, then the substitution value would be determined by the intersection of the row with index '5' and the column with index '3' in Fig. 7. This would result in $s'_{1,1}$ having a value of {ed}.

		y															
		0	1	2	3	4	5	6	7	8	9	a	b	c	d	e	f
	0	63	7c	77	7b	f2	6b	6f	c5	30	01	67	2b	fe	d7	ab	76
	1	ca	82	c9	7d	fa	59	47	f0	ad	d4	a2	af	9c	a4	72	c0
	2	b7	fd	93	26	36	3f	f7	cc	34	a5	e5	f1	71	d8	31	15
	3	04	c7	23	c3	18	96	05	9a	07	12	80	e2	eb	27	b2	75
	4	09	83	2c	1a	1b	6e	5a	a0	52	3b	d6	b3	29	e3	2f	84
	5	53	d1	00	ed	20	fc	b1	5b	6a	cb	be	39	4a	4c	58	cf
	6	d0	ef	aa	fb	43	4d	33	85	45	f9	02	7f	50	3c	9f	a8
	7	51	a3	40	8f	92	9d	38	f5	bc	b6	da	21	10	ff	f3	d2
x	8	cd	0c	13	ec	5f	97	44	17	c4	a7	7e	3d	64	5d	19	73
	9	60	81	4f	dc	22	2a	90	88	46	ee	b8	14	de	5e	0b	db
	a	e0	32	3a	0a	49	06	24	5c	c2	d3	ac	62	91	95	e4	79
	b	e7	c8	37	6d	8d	d5	4e	a9	6c	56	f4	ea	65	7a	ae	08
	c	ba	78	25	2e	1c	a6	b4	c6	e8	dd	74	1f	4b	bd	8b	8a
	d	70	3e	b5	66	48	03	f6	0e	61	35	57	b9	86	c1	1d	9e
	e	e1	f8	98	11	69	d9	8e	94	9b	1e	87	e9	ce	55	28	df
	f	8c	a1	89	0d	bf	e6	42	68	41	99	2d	0f	b0	54	bb	16

Figure 7. S-box: substitution values for the byte `xy` (in hexadecimal format).

5.1.2 `ShiftRows()` Transformation

In the **`ShiftRows()`** transformation, the bytes in the last three rows of the State are cyclically shifted over different numbers of bytes (offsets). The first row, $r = 0$, is not shifted.

Specifically, the **`ShiftRows()`** transformation proceeds as follows:

$$s'_{r,c} = s_{r,(c+shift(r,Nb)) \bmod Nb} \quad \text{for } 0 < r < 4 \quad \text{and} \quad 0 \le c < \boldsymbol{Nb}, \tag{5.3}$$

where the shift value $shift(r,Nb)$ depends on the row number, r, as follows (recall that $\boldsymbol{Nb} = 4$):

$$shift(1,4) = 1; \quad shift(2,4) = 2; \quad shift(3,4) = 3. \tag{5.4}$$

This has the effect of moving bytes to "lower" positions in the row (i.e., lower values of c in a given row), while the "lowest" bytes wrap around into the "top" of the row (i.e., higher values of c in a given row).

Figure 8 illustrates the **`ShiftRows()`** transformation.

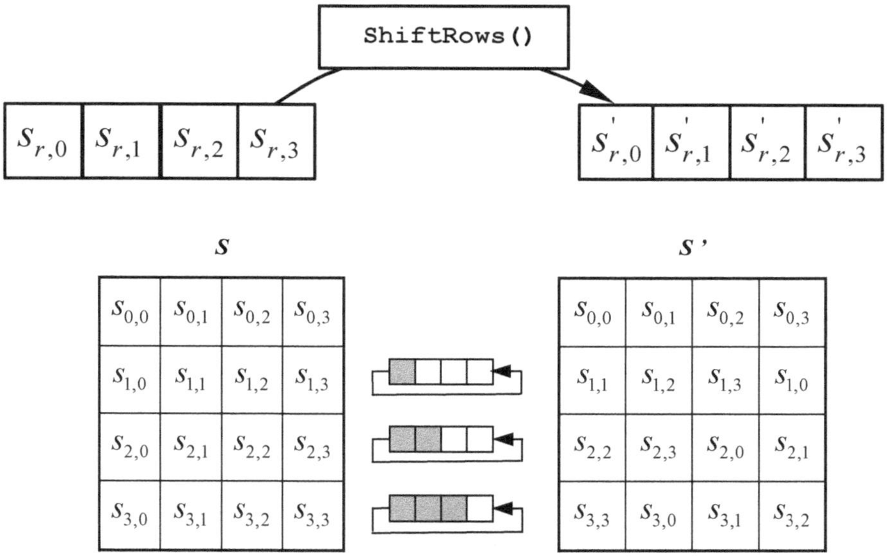

Figure 8. `ShiftRows()` cyclically shifts the last three rows in the State.

5.1.3 `MixColumns()` Transformation

The **`MixColumns()`** transformation operates on the State column-by-column, treating each column as a four-term polynomial as described in Sec. 4.3. The columns are considered as polynomials over GF(2^8) and multiplied modulo $x^4 + 1$ with a fixed polynomial $a(x)$, given by

$$a(x) = \{03\}x^3 + \{01\}x^2 + \{01\}x + \{02\}. \tag{5.5}$$

As described in Sec. 4.3, this can be written as a matrix multiplication. Let

$s'(x) = a(x) \otimes s(x)$:

$$\begin{bmatrix} s'_{0,c} \\ s'_{1,c} \\ s'_{2,c} \\ s'_{3,c} \end{bmatrix} = \begin{bmatrix} 02 & 03 & 01 & 01 \\ 01 & 02 & 03 & 01 \\ 01 & 01 & 02 & 03 \\ 03 & 01 & 01 & 02 \end{bmatrix} \begin{bmatrix} s_{0,c} \\ s_{1,c} \\ s_{2,c} \\ s_{3,c} \end{bmatrix} \quad \text{for } 0 \le c < \boldsymbol{Nb}. \tag{5.6}$$

As a result of this multiplication, the four bytes in a column are replaced by the following:

$$s'_{0,c} = (\{02\} \bullet s_{0,c}) \oplus (\{03\} \bullet s_{1,c}) \oplus s_{2,c} \oplus s_{3,c}$$

$$s'_{1,c} = s_{0,c} \oplus (\{02\} \bullet s_{1,c}) \oplus (\{03\} \bullet s_{2,c}) \oplus s_{3,c}$$

$$s'_{2,c} = s_{0,c} \oplus s_{1,c} \oplus (\{02\} \bullet s_{2,c}) \oplus (\{03\} \bullet s_{3,c})$$

$$s'_{3,c} = (\{03\} \bullet s_{0,c}) \oplus s_{1,c} \oplus s_{2,c} \oplus (\{02\} \bullet s_{3,c}).$$

Figure 9 illustrates the **`MixColumns()`** transformation.

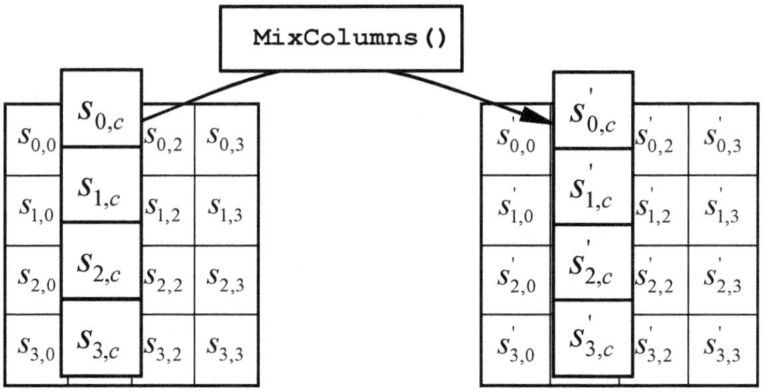

Figure 9. `MixColumns()` operates on the State column-by-column.

5.1.4 `AddRoundKey()` Transformation

In the **`AddRoundKey()`** transformation, a Round Key is added to the State by a simple bitwise XOR operation. Each Round Key consists of ***Nb*** words from the key schedule (described in Sec. 5.2). Those ***Nb*** words are each added into the columns of the State, such that

$$[s'_{0,c}, s'_{1,c}, s'_{2,c}, s'_{3,c}] = [s_{0,c}, s_{1,c}, s_{2,c}, s_{3,c}] \oplus [w_{round*Nb+c}] \quad \text{for } 0 \le c < \boldsymbol{Nb}, \tag{5.7}$$

where $[w_i]$ are the key schedule words described in Sec. 5.2, and *round* is a value in the range $0 \le round \le \boldsymbol{Nr}$. In the Cipher, the initial Round Key addition occurs when *round* = 0, prior to the first application of the round function (see Fig. 5). The application of the **`AddRoundKey()`** transformation to the ***Nr*** rounds of the Cipher occurs when $1 \le round \le \boldsymbol{Nr}$.

The action of this transformation is illustrated in Fig. 10, where l = *round* * ***Nb***. The byte address within words of the key schedule was described in Sec. 3.1.

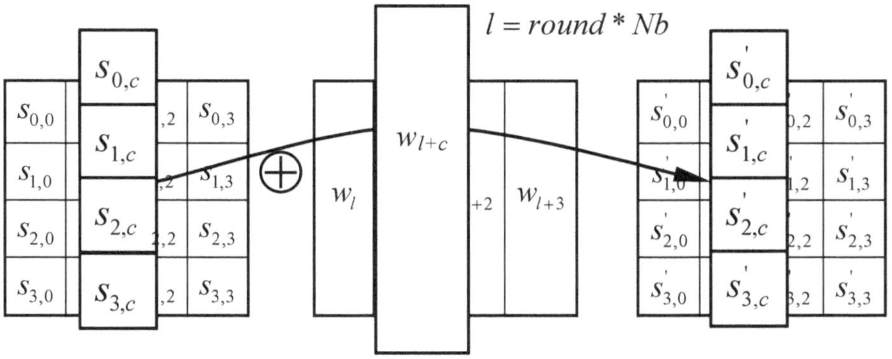

Figure 10. `AddRoundKey()` XORs each column of the State with a word from the key schedule.

5.2 Key Expansion

The AES algorithm takes the Cipher Key, ***K***, and performs a Key Expansion routine to generate a key schedule. The Key Expansion generates a total of ***Nb*** (***Nr*** + 1) words: the algorithm requires an initial set of ***Nb*** words, and each of the ***Nr*** rounds requires ***Nb*** words of key data. The resulting key schedule consists of a linear array of 4-byte words, denoted $[w_i]$, with i in the range $0 \le i < Nb(Nr + 1)$.

The expansion of the input key into the key schedule proceeds according to the pseudo code in Fig. 11.

`SubWord()` is a function that takes a four-byte input word and applies the S-box (Sec. 5.1.1, Fig. 7) to each of the four bytes to produce an output word. The function **`RotWord()`** takes a word $[a_0,a_1,a_2,a_3]$ as input, performs a cyclic permutation, and returns the word $[a_1,a_2,a_3,a_0]$. The round constant word array, **`Rcon[i]`**, contains the values given by $[x^{i-1}$,{00},{00},{00}], with x^{i-1} being powers of x (x is denoted as {02}) in the field GF(2^8), as discussed in Sec. 4.2 (note that i starts at 1, not 0).

From Fig. 11, it can be seen that the first ***Nk*** words of the expanded key are filled with the Cipher Key. Every following word, **`w[i]`**, is equal to the XOR of the previous word, **`w[i-1]`**, and the word ***Nk*** positions earlier, **`w[i-`*Nk*`]`**. For words in positions that are a multiple of ***Nk***, a transformation is applied to **`w[i-1]`** prior to the XOR, followed by an XOR with a round constant, **`Rcon[i]`**. This transformation consists of a cyclic shift of the bytes in a word (**`RotWord()`**), followed by the application of a table lookup to all four bytes of the word (**`SubWord()`**).

It is important to note that the Key Expansion routine for 256-bit Cipher Keys (***Nk*** = 8) is slightly different than for 128- and 192-bit Cipher Keys. If ***Nk*** = 8 and `i-4` is a multiple of ***Nk***, then **`SubWord()`** is applied to **`w[i-1]`** prior to the XOR.

```
KeyExpansion(byte key[4*Nk], word w[Nb*(Nr+1)], Nk)
begin
   word  temp

   i = 0

   while (i < Nk)
      w[i] = word(key[4*i], key[4*i+1], key[4*i+2], key[4*i+3])
      i = i+1
   end while

   i = Nk

   while (i < Nb * (Nr+1)]
      temp = w[i-1]
      if (i mod Nk = 0)
         temp = SubWord(RotWord(temp)) xor Rcon[i/Nk]
      else if (Nk > 6 and i mod Nk = 4)
         temp = SubWord(temp)
      end if
      w[i] = w[i-Nk] xor temp
      i = i + 1
   end while
end

Note that Nk=4, 6, and 8 do not all have to be implemented;
they are all included in the conditional statement above for
conciseness.   Specific implementation requirements for the
Cipher Key are presented in Sec. 6.1.
```

Figure 11. Pseudo Code for Key Expansion.[2]

Appendix A presents examples of the Key Expansion.

5.3 Inverse Cipher

The Cipher transformations in Sec. 5.1 can be inverted and then implemented in reverse order to produce a straightforward Inverse Cipher for the AES algorithm. The individual transformations used in the Inverse Cipher - **`InvShiftRows()`**, **`InvSubBytes()`**,**`InvMixColumns()`**, and **`AddRoundKey()`** – process the State and are described in the following subsections.

The Inverse Cipher is described in the pseudo code in Fig. 12. In Fig. 12, the array **`w[]`** contains the key schedule, which was described previously in Sec. 5.2.

[2] The functions **`SubWord()`** and **`RotWord()`** return a result that is a transformation of the function input, whereas the transformations in the Cipher and Inverse Cipher (e.g., **`ShiftRows()`**, **`SubBytes()`**, etc.) transform the State array that is addressed by the '`state`' pointer.

```
InvCipher(byte in[4*Nb], byte out[4*Nb], word w[Nb*(Nr+1)])
begin
   byte  state[4,Nb]

   state = in

   AddRoundKey(state, w[Nr*Nb, (Nr+1)*Nb-1]) // See Sec. 5.1.4

   for round = Nr-1 step -1 downto 1
      InvShiftRows(state)                    // See Sec. 5.3.1
      InvSubBytes(state)                     // See Sec. 5.3.2
      AddRoundKey(state, w[round*Nb, (round+1)*Nb-1])
      InvMixColumns(state)                   // See Sec. 5.3.3
   end for

   InvShiftRows(state)
   InvSubBytes(state)
   AddRoundKey(state, w[0, Nb-1])

   out = state
end
```

Figure 12. Pseudo Code for the Inverse Cipher.[3]

5.3.1 `InvShiftRows()` Transformation

`InvShiftRows()` is the inverse of the **`ShiftRows()`** transformation. The bytes in the last three rows of the State are cyclically shifted over different numbers of bytes (offsets). The first row, $r = 0$, is not shifted. The bottom three rows are cyclically shifted by $\boldsymbol{Nb} - \mathit{shift}(r, Nb)$ bytes, where the shift value *shift(r,Nb)* depends on the row number, and is given in equation (5.4) (see Sec. 5.1.2).

Specifically, the **`InvShiftRows()`** transformation proceeds as follows:

$$s'_{r,(c+\mathit{shift}(r,Nb)) \bmod Nb} = s_{r,c} \quad \text{for } 0 < r < 4 \quad \text{and} \quad 0 \le c < \boldsymbol{Nb} \tag{5.8}$$

Figure 13 illustrates the **`InvShiftRows()`** transformation.

[3] The various transformations (e.g., **`InvSubBytes()`**, **`InvShiftRows()`**, etc.) act upon the State array that is addressed by the '`state`' pointer. **`AddRoundKey()`** uses an additional pointer to address the Round Key.

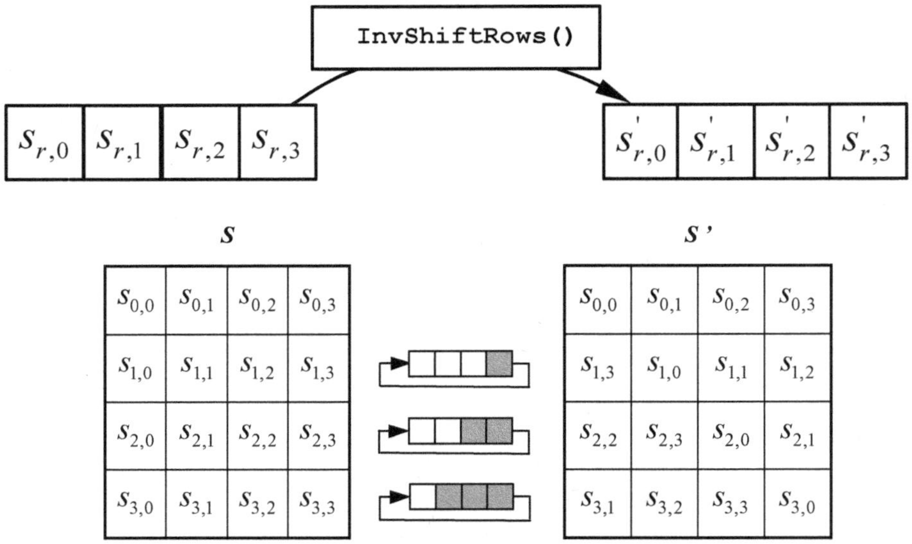

Figure 13. `InvShiftRows()` cyclically shifts the last three rows in the State.

5.3.2 `InvSubBytes()` Transformation

`InvSubBytes()` is the inverse of the byte substitution transformation, in which the inverse S-box is applied to each byte of the State. This is obtained by applying the inverse of the affine transformation (5.1) followed by taking the multiplicative inverse in GF(2^8).

The inverse S-box used in the **`InvSubBytes()`** transformation is presented in Fig. 14:

		y															
		0	1	2	3	4	5	6	7	8	9	a	b	c	d	e	f
x	0	52	09	6a	d5	30	36	a5	38	bf	40	a3	9e	81	f3	d7	fb
	1	7c	e3	39	82	9b	2f	ff	87	34	8e	43	44	c4	de	e9	cb
	2	54	7b	94	32	a6	c2	23	3d	ee	4c	95	0b	42	fa	c3	4e
	3	08	2e	a1	66	28	d9	24	b2	76	5b	a2	49	6d	8b	d1	25
	4	72	f8	f6	64	86	68	98	16	d4	a4	5c	cc	5d	65	b6	92
	5	6c	70	48	50	fd	ed	b9	da	5e	15	46	57	a7	8d	9d	84
	6	90	d8	ab	00	8c	bc	d3	0a	f7	e4	58	05	b8	b3	45	06
	7	d0	2c	1e	8f	ca	3f	0f	02	c1	af	bd	03	01	13	8a	6b
	8	3a	91	11	41	4f	67	dc	ea	97	f2	cf	ce	f0	b4	e6	73
	9	96	ac	74	22	e7	ad	35	85	e2	f9	37	e8	1c	75	df	6e
	a	47	f1	1a	71	1d	29	c5	89	6f	b7	62	0e	aa	18	be	1b
	b	fc	56	3e	4b	c6	d2	79	20	9a	db	c0	fe	78	cd	5a	f4
	c	1f	dd	a8	33	88	07	c7	31	b1	12	10	59	27	80	ec	5f
	d	60	51	7f	a9	19	b5	4a	0d	2d	e5	7a	9f	93	c9	9c	ef
	e	a0	e0	3b	4d	ae	2a	f5	b0	c8	eb	bb	3c	83	53	99	61
	f	17	2b	04	7e	ba	77	d6	26	e1	69	14	63	55	21	0c	7d

Figure 14. Inverse S-box: substitution values for the byte `xy` (in hexadecimal format).

5.3.3 **InvMixColumns()** Transformation

InvMixColumns() is the inverse of the **MixColumns()** transformation. **InvMixColumns()** operates on the State column-by-column, treating each column as a four-term polynomial as described in Sec. 4.3. The columns are considered as polynomials over GF(2^8) and multiplied modulo $x^4 + 1$ with a fixed polynomial $a^{-1}(x)$, given by

$$a^{-1}(x) = \{\texttt{0b}\}x^3 + \{\texttt{0d}\}x^2 + \{\texttt{09}\}x + \{\texttt{0e}\}. \qquad (5.9)$$

As described in Sec. 4.3, this can be written as a matrix multiplication. Let

$s'(x) = a^{-1}(x) \otimes s(x)$:

$$\begin{bmatrix} s'_{0,c} \\ s'_{1,c} \\ s'_{2,c} \\ s'_{3,c} \end{bmatrix} = \begin{bmatrix} 0e & 0b & 0d & 09 \\ 09 & 0e & 0b & 0d \\ 0d & 09 & 0e & 0b \\ 0b & 0d & 09 & 0e \end{bmatrix} \begin{bmatrix} s_{0,c} \\ s_{1,c} \\ s_{2,c} \\ s_{3,c} \end{bmatrix} \quad \text{for } 0 \le c < \boldsymbol{Nb}. \qquad (5.10)$$

As a result of this multiplication, the four bytes in a column are replaced by the following:

$$s'_{0,c} = (\{\texttt{0e}\} \bullet s_{0,c}) \oplus (\{\texttt{0b}\} \bullet s_{1,c}) \oplus (\{\texttt{0d}\} \bullet s_{2,c}) \oplus (\{\texttt{09}\} \bullet s_{3,c})$$

$$s'_{1,c} = (\{\texttt{09}\} \bullet s_{0,c}) \oplus (\{\texttt{0e}\} \bullet s_{1,c}) \oplus (\{\texttt{0b}\} \bullet s_{2,c}) \oplus (\{\texttt{0d}\} \bullet s_{3,c})$$

$$s'_{2,c} = (\{\texttt{0d}\} \bullet s_{0,c}) \oplus (\{\texttt{09}\} \bullet s_{1,c}) \oplus (\{\texttt{0e}\} \bullet s_{2,c}) \oplus (\{\texttt{0b}\} \bullet s_{3,c})$$

$$s'_{3,c} = (\{\texttt{0b}\} \bullet s_{0,c}) \oplus (\{\texttt{0d}\} \bullet s_{1,c}) \oplus (\{\texttt{09}\} \bullet s_{2,c}) \oplus (\{\texttt{0e}\} \bullet s_{3,c})$$

5.3.4 Inverse of the **AddRoundKey()** Transformation

AddRoundKey(), which was described in Sec. 5.1.4, is its own inverse, since it only involves an application of the XOR operation.

5.3.5 Equivalent Inverse Cipher

In the straightforward Inverse Cipher presented in Sec. 5.3 and Fig. 12, the sequence of the transformations differs from that of the Cipher, while the form of the key schedules for encryption and decryption remains the same. However, several properties of the AES algorithm allow for an Equivalent Inverse Cipher that has the same sequence of transformations as the Cipher (with the transformations replaced by their inverses). This is accomplished with a change in the key schedule.

The two properties that allow for this Equivalent Inverse Cipher are as follows:

1. The **SubBytes()** and **ShiftRows()** transformations commute; that is, a **SubBytes()** transformation immediately followed by a **ShiftRows()** transformation is equivalent to a **ShiftRows()** transformation immediately followed buy a **SubBytes()** transformation. The same is true for their inverses, **InvSubBytes()** and **InvShiftRows.**

2. The column mixing operations - **MixColumns()** and **InvMixColumns()** - are linear with respect to the column input, which means

```
InvMixColumns(state XOR Round Key) =
                    InvMixColumns(state) XOR InvMixColumns(Round Key).
```

These properties allow the order of **InvSubBytes()** and **InvShiftRows()** transformations to be reversed. The order of the **AddRoundKey()** and **InvMixColumns()** transformations can also be reversed, provided that the columns (words) of the decryption key schedule are modified using the **InvMixColumns()** transformation.

The equivalent inverse cipher is defined by reversing the order of the **InvSubBytes()** and **InvShiftRows()** transformations shown in Fig. 12, and by reversing the order of the **AddRoundKey()** and **InvMixColumns()** transformations used in the "round loop" after first modifying the decryption key schedule for *round* = 1 to *Nr*-1 using the **InvMixColumns()** transformation. The first and last *Nb* words of the decryption key schedule shall *not* be modified in this manner.

Given these changes, the resulting Equivalent Inverse Cipher offers a more efficient structure than the Inverse Cipher described in Sec. 5.3 and Fig. 12. Pseudo code for the Equivalent Inverse Cipher appears in Fig. 15. (The word array **dw[]** contains the modified decryption key schedule. The modification to the Key Expansion routine is also provided in Fig. 15.)

```
EqInvCipher(byte in[4*Nb], byte out[4*Nb], word dw[Nb*(Nr+1)])
begin
   byte  state[4,Nb]

   state = in

   AddRoundKey(state, dw[Nr*Nb, (Nr+1)*Nb-1])

   for round = Nr-1 step -1 downto 1
      InvSubBytes(state)
      InvShiftRows(state)
      InvMixColumns(state)
      AddRoundKey(state, dw[round*Nb, (round+1)*Nb-1])
   end for

   InvSubBytes(state)
   InvShiftRows(state)
   AddRoundKey(state, dw[0, Nb-1])

   out = state
end


For the Equivalent Inverse Cipher, the following pseudo code is added at
the end of the Key Expansion routine (Sec. 5.2):

   for i = 0 step 1 to (Nr+1)*Nb-1
      dw[i] = w[i]
   end for


   for round = 1 step 1 to Nr-1
      InvMixColumns(dw[round*Nb, (round+1)*Nb-1])      //  note  change  of
type
   end for

Note that, since InvMixColumns operates on a two-dimensional array of bytes
while the Round Keys are held in an array of words, the call to
InvMixColumns in this code sequence involves a change of type (i.e. the
input to InvMixColumns() is normally the State array, which is considered
to be a two-dimensional array of bytes, whereas the input here is a Round
Key computed as a one-dimensional array of words).
```

Figure 15. Pseudo Code for the Equivalent Inverse Cipher.

6. Implementation Issues

6.1 Key Length Requirements

An implementation of the AES algorithm shall support *at least one* of the three key lengths specified in Sec. 5: 128, 192, or 256 bits (i.e., $\boldsymbol{Nk}$ = 4, 6, or 8, respectively). Implementations may optionally support two or three key lengths, which may promote the interoperability of algorithm implementations.

6.2 Keying Restrictions

No weak or semi-weak keys have been identified for the AES algorithm, and there is no restriction on key selection.

6.3 Parameterization of Key Length, Block Size, and Round Number

This standard explicitly defines the allowed values for the key length (***Nk***), block size (***Nb***), and number of rounds (***Nr***) – see Fig. 4. However, future reaffirmations of this standard could include changes or additions to the allowed values for those parameters. Therefore, implementers may choose to design their AES implementations with future flexibility in mind.

6.4 Implementation Suggestions Regarding Various Platforms

Implementation variations are possible that may, in many cases, offer performance or other advantages. Given the same input key and data (plaintext or ciphertext), any implementation that produces the same output (ciphertext or plaintext) as the algorithm specified in this standard is an acceptable implementation of the AES.

Reference [3] and other papers located at Ref. [1] include suggestions on how to efficiently implement the AES algorithm on a variety of platforms.

Appendix A - Key Expansion Examples

This appendix shows the development of the key schedule for various key sizes. Note that multi-byte values are presented using the notation described in Sec. 3. The intermediate values produced during the development of the key schedule (see Sec. 5.2) are given in the following table (all values are in hexadecimal format, with the exception of the index column (i)).

A.1 Expansion of a 128-bit Cipher Key

This section contains the key expansion of the following cipher key:

```
Cipher Key = 2b 7e 15 16 28 ae d2 a6 ab f7 15 88 09 cf 4f 3c
```

for $Nk = 4$, which results in

$w_0 =$ 2b7e1516 $w_1 =$ 28aed2a6 $w_2 =$ abf71588 $w_3 =$ 09cf4f3c

i (dec)	temp	After RotWord()	After SubWord()	Rcon[i/Nk]	After XOR with Rcon	w[i-Nk]	w[i]= temp XOR w[i-Nk]
4	09cf4f3c	cf4f3c09	8a84eb01	01000000	8b84eb01	2b7e1516	a0fafe17
5	a0fafe17					28aed2a6	88542cb1
6	88542cb1					abf71588	23a33939
7	23a33939					09cf4f3c	2a6c7605
8	2a6c7605	6c76052a	50386be5	02000000	52386be5	a0fafe17	f2c295f2
9	f2c295f2					88542cb1	7a96b943
10	7a96b943					23a33939	5935807a
11	5935807a					2a6c7605	7359f67f
12	7359f67f	59f67f73	cb42d28f	04000000	cf42d28f	f2c295f2	3d80477d
13	3d80477d					7a96b943	4716fe3e
14	4716fe3e					5935807a	1e237e44
15	1e237e44					7359f67f	6d7a883b
16	6d7a883b	7a883b6d	dac4e23c	08000000	d2c4e23c	3d80477d	ef44a541
17	ef44a541					4716fe3e	a8525b7f
18	a8525b7f					1e237e44	b671253b
19	b671253b					6d7a883b	db0bad00
20	db0bad00	0bad00db	2b9563b9	10000000	3b9563b9	ef44a541	d4d1c6f8
21	d4d1c6f8					a8525b7f	7c839d87
22	7c839d87					b671253b	caf2b8bc
23	caf2b8bc					db0bad00	11f915bc

24	11f915bc	f915bc11	99596582	20000000	b9596582	d4d1c6f8	6d88a37a
25	6d88a37a					7c839d87	110b3efd
26	110b3efd					caf2b8bc	dbf98641
27	dbf98641					11f915bc	ca0093fd
28	ca0093fd	0093fdca	63dc5474	40000000	23dc5474	6d88a37a	4e54f70e
29	4e54f70e					110b3efd	5f5fc9f3
30	5f5fc9f3					dbf98641	84a64fb2
31	84a64fb2					ca0093fd	4ea6dc4f
32	4ea6dc4f	a6dc4f4e	2486842f	80000000	a486842f	4e54f70e	ead27321
33	ead27321					5f5fc9f3	b58dbad2
34	b58dbad2					84a64fb2	312bf560
35	312bf560					4ea6dc4f	7f8d292f
36	7f8d292f	8d292f7f	5da515d2	1b000000	46a515d2	ead27321	ac7766f3
37	ac7766f3					b58dbad2	19fadc21
38	19fadc21					312bf560	28d12941
39	28d12941					7f8d292f	575c006e
40	575c006e	5c006e57	4a639f5b	36000000	7c639f5b	ac7766f3	d014f9a8
41	d014f9a8					19fadc21	c9ee2589
42	c9ee2589					28d12941	e13f0cc8
43	e13f0cc8					575c006e	b6630ca6

A.2 Expansion of a 192-bit Cipher Key

This section contains the key expansion of the following cipher key:

```
Cipher Key =     8e 73 b0 f7 da 0e 64 52 c8 10 f3 2b
                 80 90 79 e5 62 f8 ea d2 52 2c 6b 7b
```

for ***Nk*** = 6, which results in

w_0 = 8e73b0f7 w_1 = da0e6452 w_2 = c810f32b w_3 = 809079e5

w_4 = 62f8ead2 w_5 = 522c6b7b

i (dec)	temp	After RotWord()	After SubWord()	Rcon[i/Nk]	After XOR with Rcon	w[i-Nk]	w[i]= temp XOR w[i-Nk]
6	522c6b7b	2c6b7b52	717f2100	01000000	707f2100	8e73b0f7	fe0c91f7
7	fe0c91f7					da0e6452	2402f5a5
8	2402f5a5					c810f32b	ec12068e

9	ec12068e					809079e5	6c827f6b
10	6c827f6b					62f8ead2	0e7a95b9
11	0e7a95b9					522c6b7b	5c56fec2
12	5c56fec2	56fec25c	b1bb254a	02000000	b3bb254a	fe0c91f7	4db7b4bd
13	4db7b4bd					2402f5a5	69b54118
14	69b54118					ec12068e	85a74796
15	85a74796					6c827f6b	e92538fd
16	e92538fd					0e7a95b9	e75fad44
17	e75fad44					5c56fec2	bb095386
18	bb095386	095386bb	01ed44ea	04000000	05ed44ea	4db7b4bd	485af057
19	485af057					69b54118	21efb14f
20	21efb14f					85a74796	a448f6d9
21	a448f6d9					e92538fd	4d6dce24
22	4d6dce24					e75fad44	aa326360
23	aa326360					bb095386	113b30e6
24	113b30e6	3b30e611	e2048e82	08000000	ea048e82	485af057	a25e7ed5
25	a25e7ed5					21efb14f	83b1cf9a
26	83b1cf9a					a448f6d9	27f93943
27	27f93943					4d6dce24	6a94f767
28	6a94f767					aa326360	c0a69407
29	c0a69407					113b30e6	d19da4e1
30	d19da4e1	9da4e1d1	5e49f83e	10000000	4e49f83e	a25e7ed5	ec1786eb
31	ec1786eb					83b1cf9a	6fa64971
32	6fa64971					27f93943	485f7032
33	485f7032					6a94f767	22cb8755
34	22cb8755					c0a69407	e26d1352
35	e26d1352					d19da4e1	33f0b7b3
36	33f0b7b3	f0b7b333	8ca96dc3	20000000	aca96dc3	ec1786eb	40beeb28
37	40beeb28					6fa64971	2f18a259
38	2f18a259					485f7032	6747d26b
39	6747d26b					22cb8755	458c553e
40	458c553e					e26d1352	a7e1466c
41	a7e1466c					33f0b7b3	9411f1df
42	9411f1df	11f1df94	82a19e22	40000000	c2a19e22	40beeb28	821f750a
43	821f750a					2f18a259	ad07d753

44	ad07d753					6747d26b	ca400538
45	ca400538					458c553e	8fcc5006
46	8fcc5006					a7e1466c	282d166a
47	282d166a					9411f1df	bc3ce7b5
48	bc3ce7b5	3ce7b5bc	eb94d565	80000000	6b94d565	821f750a	e98ba06f
49	e98ba06f					ad07d753	448c773c
50	448c773c					ca400538	8ecc7204
51	8ecc7204					8fcc5006	01002202

A.3 Expansion of a 256-bit Cipher Key

This section contains the key expansion of the following cipher key:

```
Cipher Key =        60 3d eb 10 15 ca 71 be 2b 73 ae f0 85 7d 77 81
                    1f 35 2c 07 3b 61 08 d7 2d 98 10 a3 09 14 df f4
```

for $Nk = 8$, which results in

w_0 = 603deb10 w_1 = 15ca71be w_2 = 2b73aef0 w_3 = 857d7781

w_4 = 1f352c07 w_5 = 3b6108d7 w_6 = 2d9810a3 w_7 = 0914dff4

i (dec)	temp	After RotWord()	After SubWord()	Rcon[i/Nk]	After XOR with Rcon	w[i-Nk]	w[i]= temp XOR w[i-Nk]
8	0914dff4	14dff409	fa9ebf01	01000000	fb9ebf01	603deb10	9ba35411
9	9ba35411					15ca71be	8e6925af
10	8e6925af					2b73aef0	a51a8b5f
11	a51a8b5f					857d7781	2067fcde
12	2067fcde		b785b01d			1f352c07	a8b09c1a
13	a8b09c1a					3b6108d7	93d194cd
14	93d194cd					2d9810a3	be49846e
15	be49846e					0914dff4	b75d5b9a
16	b75d5b9a	5d5b9ab7	4c39b8a9	02000000	4e39b8a9	9ba35411	d59aecb8
17	d59aecb8					8e6925af	5bf3c917
18	5bf3c917					a51a8b5f	fee94248
19	fee94248					2067fcde	de8ebe96
20	de8ebe96		1d19ae90			a8b09c1a	b5a9328a
21	b5a9328a					93d194cd	2678a647
22	2678a647					be49846e	98312229

23	98312229					b75d5b9a	2f6c79b3
24	2f6c79b3	6c79b32f	50b66d15	04000000	54b66d15	d59aecb8	812c81ad
25	812c81ad					5bf3c917	dadf48ba
26	dadf48ba					fee94248	24360af2
27	24360af2					de8ebe96	fab8b464
28	fab8b464		2d6c8d43			b5a9328a	98c5bfc9
29	98c5bfc9					2678a647	bebd198e
30	bebd198e					98312229	268c3ba7
31	268c3ba7					2f6c79b3	09e04214
32	09e04214	e0421409	e12cfa01	08000000	e92cfa01	812c81ad	68007bac
33	68007bac					dadf48ba	b2df3316
34	b2df3316					24360af2	96e939e4
35	96e939e4					fab8b464	6c518d80
36	6c518d80		50d15dcd			98c5bfc9	c814e204
37	c814e204					bebd198e	76a9fb8a
38	76a9fb8a					268c3ba7	5025c02d
39	5025c02d					09e04214	59c58239
40	59c58239	c5823959	a61312cb	10000000	b61312cb	68007bac	de136967
41	de136967					b2df3316	6ccc5a71
42	6ccc5a71					96e939e4	fa256395
43	fa256395					6c518d80	9674ee15
44	9674ee15		90922859			c814e204	5886ca5d
45	5886ca5d					76a9fb8a	2e2f31d7
46	2e2f31d7					5025c02d	7e0af1fa
47	7e0af1fa					59c58239	27cf73c3
48	27cf73c3	cf73c327	8a8f2ecc	20000000	aa8f2ecc	de136967	749c47ab
49	749c47ab					6ccc5a71	18501dda
50	18501dda					fa256395	e2757e4f
51	e2757e4f					9674ee15	7401905a
52	7401905a		927c60be			5886ca5d	cafaaae3
53	cafaaae3					2e2f31d7	e4d59b34
54	e4d59b34					7e0af1fa	9adf6ace
55	9adf6ace					27cf73c3	bd10190d
56	bd10190d	10190dbd	cad4d77a	40000000	8ad4d77a	749c47ab	fe4890d1
57	fe4890d1					18501dda	e6188d0b

58	e6188d0b					e2757e4f	046df344
59	046df344					7401905a	706c631e

Appendix B – Cipher Example

The following diagram shows the values in the State array as the Cipher progresses for a block length and a Cipher Key length of 16 bytes each (i.e., $Nb = 4$ and $Nk = 4$).

```
Input =        32 43 f6 a8 88 5a 30 8d 31 31 98 a2 e0 37 07 34
Cipher Key = 2b 7e 15 16 28 ae d2 a6 ab f7 15 88 09 cf 4f 3c
```

The Round Key values are taken from the Key Expansion example in Appendix A.

Round Number	Start of Round	After SubBytes	After ShiftRows	After MixColumns		Round Key Value	
	32 88 31 e0					2b 28 ab 09	
input	43 5a 31 37				⊕	7e ae f7 cf	=
	f6 30 98 07					15 d2 15 4f	
	a8 8d a2 34					16 a6 88 3c	
	19 a0 9a e9	d4 e0 b8 1e	d4 e0 b8 1e	04 e0 48 28		a0 88 23 2a	
1	3d f4 c6 f8	27 bf b4 41	bf b4 41 27	66 cb f8 06	⊕	fa 54 a3 6c	=
	e3 e2 8d 48	11 98 5d 52	5d 52 11 98	81 19 d3 26		fe 2c 39 76	
	be 2b 2a 08	ae f1 e5 30	30 ae f1 e5	e5 9a 7a 4c		17 b1 39 05	
	a4 68 6b 02	49 45 7f 77	49 45 7f 77	58 1b db 1b		f2 7a 59 73	
2	9c 9f 5b 6a	de db 39 02	db 39 02 de	4d 4b e7 6b	⊕	c2 96 35 59	=
	7f 35 ea 50	d2 96 87 53	87 53 d2 96	ca 5a ca b0		95 b9 80 f6	
	f2 2b 43 49	89 f1 1a 3b	3b 89 f1 1a	f1 ac a8 e5		f2 43 7a 7f	
	aa 61 82 68	ac ef 13 45	ac ef 13 45	75 20 53 bb		3d 47 1e 6d	
3	8f dd d2 32	73 c1 b5 23	c1 b5 23 73	ec 0b c0 25	⊕	80 16 23 7a	=
	5f e3 4a 46	cf 11 d6 5a	d6 5a cf 11	09 63 cf d0		47 fe 7e 88	
	03 ef d2 9a	7b df b5 b8	b8 7b df b5	93 33 7c dc		7d 3e 44 3b	
	48 67 4d d6	52 85 e3 f6	52 85 e3 f6	0f 60 6f 5e		ef a8 b6 db	
4	6c 1d e3 5f	50 a4 11 cf	a4 11 cf 50	d6 31 c0 b3	⊕	44 52 71 0b	=
	4e 9d b1 58	2f 5e c8 6a	c8 6a 2f 5e	da 38 10 13		a5 5b 25 ad	
	ee 0d 38 e7	28 d7 07 94	94 28 d7 07	a9 bf 6b 01		41 7f 3b 00	
	e0 c8 d9 85	e1 e8 35 97	e1 e8 35 97	25 bd b6 4c		d4 7c ca 11	
5	92 63 b1 b8	4f fb c8 6c	fb c8 6c 4f	d1 11 3a 4c	⊕	d1 83 f2 f9	=
	7f 63 35 be	d2 fb 96 ae	96 ae d2 fb	a9 d1 33 c0		c6 9d b8 15	
	e8 c0 50 01	9b ba 53 7c	7c 9b ba 53	ad 68 8e b0		f8 87 bc bc	

	f1	c1	7c	5d	a1	78	10	4c	a1	78	10	4c	4b	2c	33	37		6d	11	db	ca	
6	00	92	c8	b5	63	4f	e8	d5	4f	e8	d5	63	86	4a	9d	d2	⊕	88	0b	f9	00	=
	6f	4c	8b	d5	a8	29	3d	03	3d	03	a8	29	8d	89	f4	18		a3	3e	86	93	
	55	ef	32	0c	fc	df	23	fe	fe	fc	df	23	6d	80	e8	d8		7a	fd	41	fd	

	26	3d	e8	fd	f7	27	9b	54	f7	27	9b	54	14	46	27	34		4e	5f	84	4e	
7	0e	41	64	d2	ab	83	43	b5	83	43	b5	ab	15	16	46	2a	⊕	54	5f	a6	a6	=
	2e	b7	72	8b	31	a9	40	3d	40	3d	31	a9	b5	15	56	d8		f7	c9	4f	dc	
	17	7d	a9	25	f0	ff	d3	3f	3f	f0	ff	d3	bf	ec	d7	43		0e	f3	b2	4f	

	5a	19	a3	7a	be	d4	0a	da	be	d4	0a	da	00	b1	54	fa		ea	b5	31	7f	
8	41	49	e0	8c	83	3b	e1	64	3b	e1	64	83	51	c8	76	1b	⊕	d2	8d	2b	8d	=
	42	dc	19	04	2c	86	d4	f2	d4	f2	2c	86	2f	89	6d	99		73	ba	f5	29	
	b1	1f	65	0c	c8	c0	4d	fe	fe	c8	c0	4d	d1	ff	cd	ea		21	d2	60	2f	

	ea	04	65	85	87	f2	4d	97	87	f2	4d	97	47	40	a3	4c		ac	19	28	57	
9	83	45	5d	96	ec	6e	4c	90	6e	4c	90	ec	37	d4	70	9f	⊕	77	fa	d1	5c	=
	5c	33	98	b0	4a	c3	46	e7	46	e7	4a	c3	94	e4	3a	42		66	dc	29	00	
	f0	2d	ad	c5	8c	d8	95	a6	a6	8c	d8	95	ed	a5	a6	bc		f3	21	41	6e	

	eb	59	8b	1b	e9	cb	3d	af	e9	cb	3d	af						d0	c9	e1	b6	
10	40	2e	a1	c3	09	31	32	2e	31	32	2e	09					⊕	14	ee	3f	63	=
	f2	38	13	42	89	07	7d	2c	7d	2c	89	07						f9	25	0c	0c	
	1e	84	e7	d2	72	5f	94	b5	b5	72	5f	94						a8	89	c8	a6	

	39	02	dc	19
output	25	dc	11	6a
	84	09	85	0b
	1d	fb	97	32

Appendix C – Example Vectors

This appendix contains example vectors, including intermediate values – for all three AES key lengths (***Nk*** = 4, 6, and 8), for the Cipher, Inverse Cipher, and Equivalent Inverse Cipher that are described in Sec. 5.1, 5.3, and 5.3.5, respectively. Additional examples may be found at [1] and [5].

All vectors are in hexadecimal notation, with each pair of characters giving a byte value in which the left character of each pair provides the bit pattern for the 4 bit group containing the higher numbered bits using the notation explained in Sec. 3.2, while the right character provides the bit pattern for the lower-numbered bits. The array index for all bytes (groups of two hexadecimal digits) within these test vectors starts at zero and increases from left to right.

```
Legend for CIPHER (ENCRYPT) (round number r = 0 to 10, 12 or 14):

   input:   cipher input
   start:   state at start of round[r]
   s_box:   state after SubBytes()
   s_row:   state after ShiftRows()
   m_col:   state after MixColumns()
   k_sch:   key schedule value for round[r]
   output:  cipher output


Legend for INVERSE CIPHER (DECRYPT) (round number r = 0 to 10, 12 or 14):
   iinput:  inverse cipher input
   istart:  state at start of round[r]
   is_box:  state after InvSubBytes()
   is_row:  state after InvShiftRows()
   ik_sch:  key schedule value for round[r]
   ik_add:  state after AddRoundKey()
   ioutput: inverse cipher output


Legend for EQUIVALENT INVERSE CIPHER (DECRYPT) (round number r = 0 to 10, 12
   or 14):

   iinput:  inverse cipher input
   istart:  state at start of round[r]
   is_box:  state after InvSubBytes()
   is_row:  state after InvShiftRows()
   im_col:  state after InvMixColumns()
   ik_sch:  key schedule value for round[r]
   ioutput: inverse cipher output
```

C.1 AES-128 (*Nk*=4, *Nr*=10)

```
PLAINTEXT:          00112233445566778899aabbccddeeff
KEY:                000102030405060708090a0b0c0d0e0f

CIPHER (ENCRYPT):
```

```
round[ 0].input    00112233445566778899aabbccddeeff
round[ 0].k_sch    000102030405060708090a0b0c0d0e0f
round[ 1].start    00102030405060708090a0b0c0d0e0f0
round[ 1].s_box    63cab7040953d051cd60e0e7ba70e18c
round[ 1].s_row    6353e08c0960e104cd70b751bacad0e7
round[ 1].m_col    5f72641557f5bc92f7be3b291db9f91a
round[ 1].k_sch    d6aa74fdd2af72fadaa678f1d6ab76fe
round[ 2].start    89d810e8855ace682d1843d8cb128fe4
round[ 2].s_box    a761ca9b97be8b45d8ad1a611fc97369
round[ 2].s_row    a7be1a6997ad739bd8c9ca451f618b61
round[ 2].m_col    ff87968431d86a51645151fa773ad009
round[ 2].k_sch    b692cf0b643dbdf1be9bc5006830b3fe
round[ 3].start    4915598f55e5d7a0daca94fa1f0a63f7
round[ 3].s_box    3b59cb73fcd90ee05774222dc067fb68
round[ 3].s_row    3bd92268fc74fb735767cbe0c0590e2d
round[ 3].m_col    4c9c1e66f771f0762c3f868e534df256
round[ 3].k_sch    b6ff744ed2c2c9bf6c590cbf0469bf41
round[ 4].start    fa636a2825b339c940668a3157244d17
round[ 4].s_box    2dfb02343f6d12dd09337ec75b36e3f0
round[ 4].s_row    2d6d7ef03f33e334093602dd5bfb12c7
round[ 4].m_col    6385b79ffc538df997be478e7547d691
round[ 4].k_sch    47f7f7bc95353e03f96c32bcfd058dfd
round[ 5].start    247240236966b3fa6ed2753288425b6c
round[ 5].s_box    36400926f9336d2d9fb59d23c42c3950
round[ 5].s_row    36339d50f9b539269f2c092dc4406d23
round[ 5].m_col    f4bcd45432e554d075f1d6c51dd03b3c
round[ 5].k_sch    3caaa3e8a99f9deb50f3af57adf622aa
round[ 6].start    c81677bc9b7ac93b25027992b0261996
round[ 6].s_box    e847f56514dadde23f77b64fe7f7d490
round[ 6].s_row    e8dab6901477d4653ff7f5e2e747dd4f
round[ 6].m_col    9816ee7400f87f556b2c049c8e5ad036
round[ 6].k_sch    5e390f7df7a69296a7553dc10aa31f6b
round[ 7].start    c62fe109f75eedc3cc79395d84f9cf5d
round[ 7].s_box    b415f8016858552e4bb6124c5f998a4c
round[ 7].s_row    b458124c68b68a014b99f82e5f15554c
round[ 7].m_col    c57e1c159a9bd286f05f4be098c63439
round[ 7].k_sch    14f9701ae35fe28c440adf4d4ea9c026
round[ 8].start    d1876c0f79c4300ab45594add66ff41f
round[ 8].s_box    3e175076b61c04678dfc2295f6a8bfc0
round[ 8].s_row    3e1c22c0b6fcbf768da85067f6170495
round[ 8].m_col    baa03de7a1f9b56ed5512cba5f414d23
round[ 8].k_sch    47438735a41c65b9e016baf4aebf7ad2
round[ 9].start    fde3bad205e5d0d73547964ef1fe37f1
round[ 9].s_box    5411f4b56bd9700e96a0902fa1bb9aa1
round[ 9].s_row    54d990a16ba09ab596bbf40ea111702f
round[ 9].m_col    e9f74eec023020f61bf2ccf2353c21c7
round[ 9].k_sch    549932d1f08557681093ed9cbe2c974e
round[10].start    bd6e7c3df2b5779e0b61216e8b10b689
round[10].s_box    7a9f102789d5f50b2beffd9f3dca4ea7
round[10].s_row    7ad5fda789ef4e272bca100b3d9ff59f
round[10].k_sch    13111d7fe3944a17f307a78b4d2b30c5
round[10].output   69c4e0d86a7b0430d8cdb78070b4c55a

INVERSE CIPHER (DECRYPT):
round[ 0].iinput   69c4e0d86a7b0430d8cdb78070b4c55a
round[ 0].ik_sch   13111d7fe3944a17f307a78b4d2b30c5
round[ 1].istart   7ad5fda789ef4e272bca100b3d9ff59f
```

```
round[ 1].is_row    7a9f102789d5f50b2beffd9f3dca4ea7
round[ 1].is_box    bd6e7c3df2b5779e0b61216e8b10b689
round[ 1].ik_sch    549932d1f08557681093ed9cbe2c974e
round[ 1].ik_add    e9f74eec023020f61bf2ccf2353c21c7
round[ 2].istart    54d990a16ba09ab596bbf40ea111702f
round[ 2].is_row    5411f4b56bd9700e96a0902fa1bb9aa1
round[ 2].is_box    fde3bad205e5d0d73547964ef1fe37f1
round[ 2].ik_sch    47438735a41c65b9e016baf4aebf7ad2
round[ 2].ik_add    baa03de7a1f9b56ed5512cba5f414d23
round[ 3].istart    3e1c22c0b6fcbf768da85067f6170495
round[ 3].is_row    3e175076b61c04678dfc2295f6a8bfc0
round[ 3].is_box    d1876c0f79c4300ab45594add66ff41f
round[ 3].ik_sch    14f9701ae35fe28c440adf4d4ea9c026
round[ 3].ik_add    c57e1c159a9bd286f05f4be098c63439
round[ 4].istart    b458124c68b68a014b99f82e5f15554c
round[ 4].is_row    b415f8016858552e4bb6124c5f998a4c
round[ 4].is_box    c62fe109f75eedc3cc79395d84f9cf5d
round[ 4].ik_sch    5e390f7df7a69296a7553dc10aa31f6b
round[ 4].ik_add    9816ee7400f87f556b2c049c8e5ad036
round[ 5].istart    e8dab6901477d4653ff7f5e2e747dd4f
round[ 5].is_row    e847f56514dadde23f77b64fe7f7d490
round[ 5].is_box    c81677bc9b7ac93b25027992b0261996
round[ 5].ik_sch    3caaa3e8a99f9deb50f3af57adf622aa
round[ 5].ik_add    f4bcd45432e554d075f1d6c51dd03b3c
round[ 6].istart    36339d50f9b539269f2c092dc4406d23
round[ 6].is_row    36400926f9336d2d9fb59d23c42c3950
round[ 6].is_box    247240236966b3fa6ed2753288425b6c
round[ 6].ik_sch    47f7f7bc95353e03f96c32bcfd058dfd
round[ 6].ik_add    6385b79ffc538df997be478e7547d691
round[ 7].istart    2d6d7ef03f33e334093602dd5bfb12c7
round[ 7].is_row    2dfb02343f6d12dd09337ec75b36e3f0
round[ 7].is_box    fa636a2825b339c940668a3157244d17
round[ 7].ik_sch    b6ff744ed2c2c9bf6c590cbf0469bf41
round[ 7].ik_add    4c9c1e66f771f0762c3f868e534df256
round[ 8].istart    3bd92268fc74fb735767cbe0c0590e2d
round[ 8].is_row    3b59cb73fcd90ee05774222dc067fb68
round[ 8].is_box    4915598f55e5d7a0daca94fa1f0a63f7
round[ 8].ik_sch    b692cf0b643dbdf1be9bc5006830b3fe
round[ 8].ik_add    ff87968431d86a51645151fa773ad009
round[ 9].istart    a7be1a6997ad739bd8c9ca451f618b61
round[ 9].is_row    a761ca9b97be8b45d8ad1a611fc97369
round[ 9].is_box    89d810e8855ace682d1843d8cb128fe4
round[ 9].ik_sch    d6aa74fdd2af72fadaa678f1d6ab76fe
round[ 9].ik_add    5f72641557f5bc92f7be3b291db9f91a
round[10].istart    6353e08c0960e104cd70b751bacad0e7
round[10].is_row    63cab7040953d051cd60e0e7ba70e18c
round[10].is_box    00102030405060708090a0b0c0d0e0f0
round[10].ik_sch    000102030405060708090a0b0c0d0e0f
round[10].ioutput   00112233445566778899aabbccddeeff

EQUIVALENT INVERSE CIPHER (DECRYPT):
round[ 0].iinput    69c4e0d86a7b0430d8cdb78070b4c55a
round[ 0].ik_sch    13111d7fe3944a17f307a78b4d2b30c5
round[ 1].istart    7ad5fda789ef4e272bca100b3d9ff59f
round[ 1].is_box    bdb52189f261b63d0b107c9e8b6e776e
round[ 1].is_row    bd6e7c3df2b5779e0b61216e8b10b689
round[ 1].im_col    4773b91ff72f354361cb018ea1e6cf2c
```

```
round[ 1].ik_sch    13aa29be9c8faff6f770f58000f7bf03
round[ 2].istart    54d990a16ba09ab596bbf40ea111702f
round[ 2].is_box    fde596f1054737d235febad7f1e3d04e
round[ 2].is_row    fde3bad205e5d0d73547964ef1fe37f1
round[ 2].im_col    2d7e86a339d9393ee6570a1101904e16
round[ 2].ik_sch    1362a4638f2586486bff5a76f7874a83
round[ 3].istart    3e1c22c0b6fcbf768da85067f6170495
round[ 3].is_box    d1c4941f7955f40fb46f6c0ad68730ad
round[ 3].is_row    d1876c0f79c4300ab45594add66ff41f
round[ 3].im_col    39daee38f4f1a82aaf432410c36d45b9
round[ 3].ik_sch    8d82fc749c47222be4dadc3e9c7810f5
round[ 4].istart    b458124c68b68a014b99f82e5f15554c
round[ 4].is_box    c65e395df779cf09ccf9e1c3842fed5d
round[ 4].is_row    c62fe109f75eedc3cc79395d84f9cf5d
round[ 4].im_col    9a39bf1d05b20a3a476a0bf79fe51184
round[ 4].ik_sch    72e3098d11c5de5f789dfe1578a2cccb
round[ 5].istart    e8dab6901477d4653ff7f5e2e747dd4f
round[ 5].is_box    c87a79969b0219bc2526773bb016c992
round[ 5].is_row    c81677bc9b7ac93b25027992b0261996
round[ 5].im_col    18f78d779a93eef4f6742967c47f5ffd
round[ 5].ik_sch    2ec410276326d7d26958204a003f32de
round[ 6].istart    36339d50f9b539269f2c092dc4406d23
round[ 6].is_box    2466756c69d25b236e4240fa8872b332
round[ 6].is_row    247240236966b3fa6ed2753288425b6c
round[ 6].im_col    85cf8bf472d124c10348f545329c0053
round[ 6].ik_sch    a8a2f5044de2c7f50a7ef79869671294
round[ 7].istart    2d6d7ef03f33e334093602dd5bfb12c7
round[ 7].is_box    fab38a1725664d2840246ac957633931
round[ 7].is_row    fa636a2825b339c940668a3157244d17
round[ 7].im_col    fc1fc1f91934c98210fbfb8da340eb21
round[ 7].ik_sch    c7c6e391e54032f1479c306d6319e50c
round[ 8].istart    3bd92268fc74fb735767cbe0c0590e2d
round[ 8].is_box    49e594f755ca638fda0a59a01f15d7fa
round[ 8].is_row    4915598f55e5d7a0daca94fa1f0a63f7
round[ 8].im_col    076518f0b52ba2fb7a15c8d93be45e00
round[ 8].ik_sch    a0db02992286d160a2dc029c2485d561
round[ 9].istart    a7be1a6997ad739bd8c9ca451f618b61
round[ 9].is_box    895a43e485188fe82d121068cbd8ced8
round[ 9].is_row    89d810e8855ace682d1843d8cb128fe4
round[ 9].im_col    ef053f7c8b3d32fd4d2a64ad3c93071a
round[ 9].ik_sch    8c56dff0825dd3f9805ad3fc8659d7fd
round[10].istart    6353e08c0960e104cd70b751bacad0e7
round[10].is_box    0050a0f04090e03080d02070c01060b0
round[10].is_row    00102030405060708090a0b0c0d0e0f0
round[10].ik_sch    000102030405060708090a0b0c0d0e0f
round[10].ioutput   00112233445566778899aabbccddeeff
```

C.2 AES-192 (*Nk*=6, *Nr*=12)

```
PLAINTEXT:  00112233445566778899aabbccddeeff
KEY:        000102030405060708090a0b0c0d0e0f1011121314151617

CIPHER (ENCRYPT):
round[ 0].input     00112233445566778899aabbccddeeff
round[ 0].k_sch     000102030405060708090a0b0c0d0e0f
round[ 1].start     00102030405060708090a0b0c0d0e0f0
```

```
round[ 1].s_box     63cab7040953d051cd60e0e7ba70e18c
round[ 1].s_row     6353e08c0960e104cd70b751bacad0e7
round[ 1].m_col     5f72641557f5bc92f7be3b291db9f91a
round[ 1].k_sch     10111213141516175846f2f95c43f4fe
round[ 2].start     4f63760643e0aa85aff8c9d041fa0de4
round[ 2].s_box     84fb386f1ae1ac977941dd70832dd769
round[ 2].s_row     84e1dd691a41d76f792d389783fbac70
round[ 2].m_col     9f487f794f955f662afc86abd7f1ab29
round[ 2].k_sch     544afef55847f0fa4856e2e95c43f4fe
round[ 3].start     cb02818c17d2af9c62aa64428bb25fd7
round[ 3].s_box     1f770c64f0b579deaaac432c3d37cf0e
round[ 3].s_row     1fb5430ef0accf64aa370cde3d77792c
round[ 3].m_col     b7a53ecbbf9d75a0c40efc79b674cc11
round[ 3].k_sch     40f949b31cbabd4d48f043b810b7b342
round[ 4].start     f75c7778a327c8ed8cfebfc1a6c37f53
round[ 4].s_box     684af5bc0acce85564bb0878242ed2ed
round[ 4].s_row     68cc08ed0abbd2bc642ef555244ae878
round[ 4].m_col     7a1e98bdacb6d1141a6944dd06eb2d3e
round[ 4].k_sch     58e151ab04a2a5557effb5416245080c
round[ 5].start     22ffc916a81474416496f19c64ae2532
round[ 5].s_box     9316dd47c2fa92834390a1de43e43f23
round[ 5].s_row     93faa123c2903f4743e4dd83431692de
round[ 5].m_col     aaa755b34cffe57cef6f98e1f01c13e6
round[ 5].k_sch     2ab54bb43a02f8f662e3a95d66410c08
round[ 6].start     80121e0776fd1d8a8d8c31bc965d1fee
round[ 6].s_box     cdc972c53854a47e5d64c765904cc028
round[ 6].s_row     cd54c7283864c0c55d4c727e90c9a465
round[ 6].m_col     921f748fd96e937d622d7725ba8ba50c
round[ 6].k_sch     f501857297448d7ebdf1c6ca87f33e3c
round[ 7].start     671ef1fd4e2a1e03dfdcb1ef3d789b30
round[ 7].s_box     8572a1542fe5727b9e86c8df27bc1404
round[ 7].s_row     85e5c8042f8614549ebca17b277272df
round[ 7].m_col     e913e7b18f507d4b227ef652758acbcc
round[ 7].k_sch     e510976183519b6934157c9ea351f1e0
round[ 8].start     0c0370d00c01e622166b8accd6db3a2c
round[ 8].s_box     fe7b5170fe7c8e93477f7e4bf6b98071
round[ 8].s_row     fe7c7e71fe7f807047b95193f67b8e4b
round[ 8].m_col     6cf5edf996eb0a069c4ef21cbfc25762
round[ 8].k_sch     1ea0372a995309167c439e77ff12051e
round[ 9].start     7255dad30fb80310e00d6c6b40d0527c
round[ 9].s_box     40fc5766766c7bcae1d7507f09700010
round[ 9].s_row     406c501076d70066e17057ca09fc7b7f
round[ 9].m_col     7478bcdce8a50b81d4327a9009188262
round[ 9].k_sch     dd7e0e887e2fff68608fc842f9dcc154
round[10].start     a906b254968af4e9b4bdb2d2f0c44336
round[10].s_box     d36f3720907ebf1e8d7a37b58c1c1a05
round[10].s_row     d37e3705907a1a208d1c371e8c6fbfb5
round[10].m_col     0d73cc2d8f6abe8b0cf2dd9bb83d422e
round[10].k_sch     859f5f237a8d5a3dc0c02952beefd63a
round[11].start     88ec930ef5e7e4b6cc32f4c906d29414
round[11].s_box     c4cedcabe694694e4b23bfdd6fb522fa
round[11].s_row     c494bffae62322ab4bb5dc4e6fce69dd
round[11].m_col     71d720933b6d677dc00b8f28238e0fb7
round[11].k_sch     de601e7827bcdf2ca223800fd8aeda32
round[12].start     afb73eeb1cd1b85162280f27fb20d585
round[12].s_box     79a9b2e99c3e6cd1aa3476cc0fb70397
round[12].s_row     793e76979c3403e9aab7b2d10fa96ccc
```

```
round[12].k_sch     a4970a331a78dc09c418c271e3a41d5d
round[12].output    dda97ca4864cdfe06eaf70a0ec0d7191

INVERSE CIPHER (DECRYPT):
round[ 0].iinput    dda97ca4864cdfe06eaf70a0ec0d7191
round[ 0].ik_sch    a4970a331a78dc09c418c271e3a41d5d
round[ 1].istart    793e76979c3403e9aab7b2d10fa96ccc
round[ 1].is_row    79a9b2e99c3e6cd1aa3476cc0fb70397
round[ 1].is_box    afb73eeb1cd1b85162280f27fb20d585
round[ 1].ik_sch    de601e7827bcdf2ca223800fd8aeda32
round[ 1].ik_add    71d720933b6d677dc00b8f28238e0fb7
round[ 2].istart    c494bffae62322ab4bb5dc4e6fce69dd
round[ 2].is_row    c4cedcabe694694e4b23bfdd6fb522fa
round[ 2].is_box    88ec930ef5e7e4b6cc32f4c906d29414
round[ 2].ik_sch    859f5f237a8d5a3dc0c02952beefd63a
round[ 2].ik_add    0d73cc2d8f6abe8b0cf2dd9bb83d422e
round[ 3].istart    d37e3705907a1a208d1c371e8c6fbfb5
round[ 3].is_row    d36f3720907ebf1e8d7a37b58c1c1a05
round[ 3].is_box    a906b254968af4e9b4bdb2d2f0c44336
round[ 3].ik_sch    dd7e0e887e2fff68608fc842f9dcc154
round[ 3].ik_add    7478bcdce8a50b81d4327a9009188262
round[ 4].istart    406c501076d70066e17057ca09fc7b7f
round[ 4].is_row    40fc5766766c7bcae1d7507f09700010
round[ 4].is_box    7255dad30fb80310e00d6c6b40d0527c
round[ 4].ik_sch    1ea0372a995309167c439e77ff12051e
round[ 4].ik_add    6cf5edf996eb0a069c4ef21cbfc25762
round[ 5].istart    fe7c7e71fe7f807047b95193f67b8e4b
round[ 5].is_row    fe7b5170fe7c8e93477f7e4bf6b98071
round[ 5].is_box    0c0370d00c01e622166b8accd6db3a2c
round[ 5].ik_sch    e510976183519b6934157c9ea351f1e0
round[ 5].ik_add    e913e7b18f507d4b227ef652758acbcc
round[ 6].istart    85e5c8042f8614549ebca17b277272df
round[ 6].is_row    8572a1542fe5727b9e86c8df27bc1404
round[ 6].is_box    671ef1fd4e2a1e03dfdcb1ef3d789b30
round[ 6].ik_sch    f501857297448d7ebdf1c6ca87f33e3c
round[ 6].ik_add    921f748fd96e937d622d7725ba8ba50c
round[ 7].istart    cd54c7283864c0c55d4c727e90c9a465
round[ 7].is_row    cdc972c53854a47e5d64c765904cc028
round[ 7].is_box    80121e0776fd1d8a8d8c31bc965d1fee
round[ 7].ik_sch    2ab54bb43a02f8f662e3a95d66410c08
round[ 7].ik_add    aaa755b34cffe57cef6f98e1f01c13e6
round[ 8].istart    93faa123c2903f4743e4dd83431692de
round[ 8].is_row    9316dd47c2fa92834390a1de43e43f23
round[ 8].is_box    22ffc916a81474416496f19c64ae2532
round[ 8].ik_sch    58e151ab04a2a5557effb5416245080c
round[ 8].ik_add    7a1e98bdacb6d1141a6944dd06eb2d3e
round[ 9].istart    68cc08ed0abbd2bc642ef555244ae878
round[ 9].is_row    684af5bc0acce85564bb0878242ed2ed
round[ 9].is_box    f75c7778a327c8ed8cfebfc1a6c37f53
round[ 9].ik_sch    40f949b31cbabd4d48f043b810b7b342
round[ 9].ik_add    b7a53ecbbf9d75a0c40efc79b674cc11
round[10].istart    1fb5430ef0accf64aa370cde3d77792c
round[10].is_row    1f770c64f0b579deaaac432c3d37cf0e
round[10].is_box    cb02818c17d2af9c62aa64428bb25fd7
round[10].ik_sch    544afef55847f0fa4856e2e95c43f4fe
round[10].ik_add    9f487f794f955f662afc86abd7f1ab29
round[11].istart    84e1dd691a41d76f792d389783fbac70
```

```
round[11].is_row   84fb386f1ae1ac977941dd70832dd769
round[11].is_box   4f63760643e0aa85aff8c9d041fa0de4
round[11].ik_sch   10111213141516175846f2f95c43f4fe
round[11].ik_add   5f72641557f5bc92f7be3b291db9f91a
round[12].istart   6353e08c0960e104cd70b751bacad0e7
round[12].is_row   63cab7040953d051cd60e0e7ba70e18c
round[12].is_box   00102030405060708090a0b0c0d0e0f0
round[12].ik_sch   000102030405060708090a0b0c0d0e0f
round[12].ioutput  00112233445566778899aabbccddeeff

EQUIVALENT INVERSE CIPHER (DECRYPT):
round[ 0].iinput   dda97ca4864cdfe06eaf70a0ec0d7191
round[ 0].ik_sch   a4970a331a78dc09c418c271e3a41d5d
round[ 1].istart   793e76979c3403e9aab7b2d10fa96ccc
round[ 1].is_box   afd10f851c28d5eb62203e51fbb7b827
round[ 1].is_row   afb73eeb1cd1b85162280f27fb20d585
round[ 1].im_col   122a02f7242ac8e20605afce51cc7264
round[ 1].ik_sch   d6bebd0dc209ea494db073803e021bb9
round[ 2].istart   c494bffae62322ab4bb5dc4e6fce69dd
round[ 2].is_box   88e7f414f532940eccd293b606ece4c9
round[ 2].is_row   88ec930ef5e7e4b6cc32f4c906d29414
round[ 2].im_col   5cc7aecce3c872194ae5ef8309a933c7
round[ 2].ik_sch   8fb999c973b26839c7f9d89d85c68c72
round[ 3].istart   d37e3705907a1a208d1c371e8c6fbfb5
round[ 3].is_box   a98ab23696bd4354b4c4b2e9f006f4d2
round[ 3].is_row   a906b254968af4e9b4bdb2d2f0c44336
round[ 3].im_col   b7113ed134e85489b20866b51d4b2c3b
round[ 3].ik_sch   f77d6ec1423f54ef5378317f14b75744
round[ 4].istart   406c501076d70066e17057ca09fc7b7f
round[ 4].is_box   72b86c7c0f0d52d3e0d0da104055036b
round[ 4].is_row   7255dad30fb80310e00d6c6b40d0527c
round[ 4].im_col   ef3b1be1b9b0e64bdcb79f1e0a707fbb
round[ 4].ik_sch   1147659047cf663b9b0ece8dfc0bf1f0
round[ 5].istart   fe7c7e71fe7f807047b95193f67b8e4b
round[ 5].is_box   0c018a2c0c6b3ad016db7022d603e6cc
round[ 5].is_row   0c0370d00c01e622166b8accd6db3a2c
round[ 5].im_col   592460b248832b2952e0b831923048f1
round[ 5].ik_sch   dcc1a8b667053f7dcc5c194ab5423a2e
round[ 6].istart   85e5c8042f8614549ebca17b277272df
round[ 6].is_box   672ab1304edc9bfddf78f1033d1e1eef
round[ 6].is_row   671ef1fd4e2a1e03dfdcb1ef3d789b30
round[ 6].im_col   0b8a7783417ae3a1f9492dc0c641a7ce
round[ 6].ik_sch   c6deb0ab791e2364a4055fbe568803ab
round[ 7].istart   cd54c7283864c0c55d4c727e90c9a465
round[ 7].is_box   80fd31ee768c1f078d5d1e8a96121dbc
round[ 7].is_row   80121e0776fd1d8a8d8c31bc965d1fee
round[ 7].im_col   4ee1ddf9301d6352c9ad769ef8d20515
round[ 7].ik_sch   dd1b7cdaf28d5c158a49ab1dbbc497cb
round[ 8].istart   93faa123c2903f4743e4dd83431692de
round[ 8].is_box   2214f132a896251664aec94164ff749c
round[ 8].is_row   22ffc916a81474416496f19c64ae2532
round[ 8].im_col   1008ffe53b36ee6af27b42549b8a7bb7
round[ 8].ik_sch   78c4f708318d3cd69655b701bfc093cf
round[ 9].istart   68cc08ed0abbd2bc642ef555244ae878
round[ 9].is_box   f727bf53a3fe7f788cc377eda65cc8c1
round[ 9].is_row   f75c7778a327c8ed8cfebfc1a6c37f53
round[ 9].im_col   7f69ac1ed939ebaac8ece3cb12e159e3
```

```
round[ 9].ik_sch    60dcef10299524ce62dbef152f9620cf
round[10].istart    1fb5430ef0accf64aa370cde3d77792c
round[10].is_box    cbd264d717aa5f8c62b2819c8b02af42
round[10].is_row    cb02818c17d2af9c62aa64428bb25fd7
round[10].im_col    cfaf16b2570c18b52e7fef50cab267ae
round[10].ik_sch    4b4ecbdb4d4dcfda5752d7c74949cbde
round[11].istart    84e1dd691a41d76f792d389783fbac70
round[11].is_box    4fe0c9e443f80d06affa76854163aad0
round[11].is_row    4f63760643e0aa85aff8c9d041fa0de4
round[11].im_col    794cf891177bfd1d8a327086f3831b39
round[11].ik_sch    1a1f181d1e1b1c194742c7d74949cbde
round[12].istart    6353e08c0960e104cd70b751bacad0e7
round[12].is_box    0050a0f04090e03080d02070c01060b0
round[12].is_row    00102030405060708090a0b0c0d0e0f0
round[12].ik_sch    000102030405060708090a0b0c0d0e0f
round[12].ioutput   00112233445566778899aabbccddeeff
```

C.3 AES-256 (Nk=8, Nr=14)

```
PLAINTEXT:    00112233445566778899aabbccddeeff
KEY:          000102030405060708090a0b0c0d0e0f101112131415161718191a1b1c1d1e1f

CIPHER (ENCRYPT):
round[ 0].input     00112233445566778899aabbccddeeff
round[ 0].k_sch     000102030405060708090a0b0c0d0e0f
round[ 1].start     00102030405060708090a0b0c0d0e0f0
round[ 1].s_box     63cab7040953d051cd60e0e7ba70e18c
round[ 1].s_row     6353e08c0960e104cd70b751bacad0e7
round[ 1].m_col     5f72641557f5bc92f7be3b291db9f91a
round[ 1].k_sch     101112131415161718191a1b1c1d1e1f
round[ 2].start     4f63760643e0aa85efa7213201a4e705
round[ 2].s_box     84fb386f1ae1ac97df5cfd237c49946b
round[ 2].s_row     84e1fd6b1a5c946fdf4938977cfbac23
round[ 2].m_col     bd2a395d2b6ac438d192443e615da195
round[ 2].k_sch     a573c29fa176c498a97fce93a572c09c
round[ 3].start     1859fbc28a1c00a078ed8aadc42f6109
round[ 3].s_box     adcb0f257e9c63e0bc557e951c15ef01
round[ 3].s_row     ad9c7e017e55ef25bc150fe01ccb6395
round[ 3].m_col     810dce0cc9db8172b3678c1e88a1b5bd
round[ 3].k_sch     1651a8cd0244beda1a5da4c10640bade
round[ 4].start     975c66c1cb9f3fa8a93a28df8ee10f63
round[ 4].s_box     884a33781fdb75c2d380349e19f876fb
round[ 4].s_row     88db34fb1f807678d3f833c2194a759e
round[ 4].m_col     b2822d81abe6fb275faf103a078c0033
round[ 4].k_sch     ae87dff00ff11b68a68ed5fb03fc1567
round[ 5].start     1c05f271a417e04ff921c5c104701554
round[ 5].s_box     9c6b89a349f0e18499fda678f2515920
round[ 5].s_row     9cf0a62049fd59a399518984f26be178
round[ 5].m_col     aeb65ba974e0f822d73f567bdb64c877
round[ 5].k_sch     6de1f1486fa54f9275f8eb5373b8518d
round[ 6].start     c357aae11b45b7b0a2c7bd28a8dc99fa
round[ 6].s_box     2e5bacf8af6ea9e73ac67a34c286ee2d
round[ 6].s_row     2e6e7a2dafc6eef83a86ace7c25ba934
round[ 6].m_col     b951c33c02e9bd29ae25cdb1efa08cc7
round[ 6].k_sch     c656827fc9a799176f294cec6cd5598b
round[ 7].start     7f074143cb4e243ec10c815d8375d54c
round[ 7].s_box     d2c5831a1f2f36b278fe0c4cec9d0329
```

```
round[ 7].s_row     d22f0c291ffe031a789d83b2ecc5364c
round[ 7].m_col     ebb19e1c3ee7c9e87d7535e9ed6b9144
round[ 7].k_sch     3de23a75524775e727bf9eb45407cf39
round[ 8].start     d653a4696ca0bc0f5acaab5db96c5e7d
round[ 8].s_box     f6ed49f950e06576be74624c565058ff
round[ 8].s_row     f6e062ff507458f9be50497656ed654c
round[ 8].m_col     5174c8669da98435a8b3e62ca974a5ea
round[ 8].k_sch     0bdc905fc27b0948ad5245a4c1871c2f
round[ 9].start     5aa858395fd28d7d05e1a38868f3b9c5
round[ 9].s_box     bec26a12cfb55dff6bf80ac4450d56a6
round[ 9].s_row     beb50aa6cff856126b0d6aff45c25dc4
round[ 9].m_col     0f77ee31d2ccadc05430a83f4ef96ac3
round[ 9].k_sch     45f5a66017b2d387300d4d33640a820a
round[10].start     4a824851c57e7e47643de50c2af3e8c9
round[10].s_box     d61352d1a6f3f3a04327d9fee50d9bdd
round[10].s_row     d6f3d9dda6279bd1430d52a0e513f3fe
round[10].m_col     bd86f0ea748fc4f4630f11c1e9331233
round[10].k_sch     7ccff71cbeb4fe5413e6bbf0d261a7df
round[11].start     c14907f6ca3b3aa070e9aa313b52b5ec
round[11].s_box     783bc54274e280e0511eacc7e200d5ce
round[11].s_row     78e2acce741ed5425100c5e0e23b80c7
round[11].m_col     af8690415d6e1dd387e5fbedd5c89013
round[11].k_sch     f01afafee7a82979d7a5644ab3afe640
round[12].start     5f9c6abfbac634aa50409fa766677653
round[12].s_box     cfde0208f4b418ac5309db5c338538ed
round[12].s_row     cfb4dbedf4093808538502ac33de185c
round[12].m_col     7427fae4d8a695269ce83d315be0392b
round[12].k_sch     2541fe719bf500258813bbd55a721c0a
round[13].start     516604954353950314fb86e401922521
round[13].s_box     d133f22a1aed2a7bfa0f44697c4f3ffd
round[13].s_row     d1ed44fd1a0f3f2afa4ff27b7c332a69
round[13].m_col     2c21a820306f154ab712c75eee0da04f
round[13].k_sch     4e5a6699a9f24fe07e572baacdf8cdea
round[14].start     627bceb9999d5aaac945ecf423f56da5
round[14].s_box     aa218b56ee5ebeacdd6ecebf26e63c06
round[14].s_row     aa5ece06ee6e3c56dde68bac2621bebf
round[14].k_sch     24fc79ccbf0979e9371ac23c6d68de36
round[14].output    8ea2b7ca516745bfeafc49904b496089

INVERSE CIPHER (DECRYPT):
round[ 0].iinput    8ea2b7ca516745bfeafc49904b496089
round[ 0].ik_sch    24fc79ccbf0979e9371ac23c6d68de36
round[ 1].istart    aa5ece06ee6e3c56dde68bac2621bebf
round[ 1].is_row    aa218b56ee5ebeacdd6ecebf26e63c06
round[ 1].is_box    627bceb9999d5aaac945ecf423f56da5
round[ 1].ik_sch    4e5a6699a9f24fe07e572baacdf8cdea
round[ 1].ik_add    2c21a820306f154ab712c75eee0da04f
round[ 2].istart    d1ed44fd1a0f3f2afa4ff27b7c332a69
round[ 2].is_row    d133f22a1aed2a7bfa0f44697c4f3ffd
round[ 2].is_box    516604954353950314fb86e401922521
round[ 2].ik_sch    2541fe719bf500258813bbd55a721c0a
round[ 2].ik_add    7427fae4d8a695269ce83d315be0392b
round[ 3].istart    cfb4dbedf4093808538502ac33de185c
round[ 3].is_row    cfde0208f4b418ac5309db5c338538ed
round[ 3].is_box    5f9c6abfbac634aa50409fa766677653
round[ 3].ik_sch    f01afafee7a82979d7a5644ab3afe640
round[ 3].ik_add    af8690415d6e1dd387e5fbedd5c89013
```

```
round[ 4].istart    78e2acce741ed5425100c5e0e23b80c7
round[ 4].is_row    783bc54274e280e0511eacc7e200d5ce
round[ 4].is_box    c14907f6ca3b3aa070e9aa313b52b5ec
round[ 4].ik_sch    7ccff71cbeb4fe5413e6bbf0d261a7df
round[ 4].ik_add    bd86f0ea748fc4f4630f11c1e9331233
round[ 5].istart    d6f3d9dda6279bd1430d52a0e513f3fe
round[ 5].is_row    d61352d1a6f3f3a04327d9fee50d9bdd
round[ 5].is_box    4a824851c57e7e47643de50c2af3e8c9
round[ 5].ik_sch    45f5a66017b2d387300d4d33640a820a
round[ 5].ik_add    0f77ee31d2ccadc05430a83f4ef96ac3
round[ 6].istart    beb50aa6cff856126b0d6aff45c25dc4
round[ 6].is_row    bec26a12cfb55dff6bf80ac4450d56a6
round[ 6].is_box    5aa858395fd28d7d05e1a38868f3b9c5
round[ 6].ik_sch    0bdc905fc27b0948ad5245a4c1871c2f
round[ 6].ik_add    5174c8669da98435a8b3e62ca974a5ea
round[ 7].istart    f6e062ff507458f9be50497656ed654c
round[ 7].is_row    f6ed49f950e06576be74624c565058ff
round[ 7].is_box    d653a4696ca0bc0f5acaab5db96c5e7d
round[ 7].ik_sch    3de23a75524775e727bf9eb45407cf39
round[ 7].ik_add    ebb19e1c3ee7c9e87d7535e9ed6b9144
round[ 8].istart    d22f0c291ffe031a789d83b2ecc5364c
round[ 8].is_row    d2c5831a1f2f36b278fe0c4cec9d0329
round[ 8].is_box    7f074143cb4e243ec10c815d8375d54c
round[ 8].ik_sch    c656827fc9a799176f294cec6cd5598b
round[ 8].ik_add    b951c33c02e9bd29ae25cdb1efa08cc7
round[ 9].istart    2e6e7a2dafc6eef83a86ace7c25ba934
round[ 9].is_row    2e5bacf8af6ea9e73ac67a34c286ee2d
round[ 9].is_box    c357aae11b45b7b0a2c7bd28a8dc99fa
round[ 9].ik_sch    6de1f1486fa54f9275f8eb5373b8518d
round[ 9].ik_add    aeb65ba974e0f822d73f567bdb64c877
round[10].istart    9cf0a62049fd59a399518984f26be178
round[10].is_row    9c6b89a349f0e18499fda678f2515920
round[10].is_box    1c05f271a417e04ff921c5c104701554
round[10].ik_sch    ae87dff00ff11b68a68ed5fb03fc1567
round[10].ik_add    b2822d81abe6fb275faf103a078c0033
round[11].istart    88db34fb1f807678d3f833c2194a759e
round[11].is_row    884a33781fdb75c2d380349e19f876fb
round[11].is_box    975c66c1cb9f3fa8a93a28df8ee10f63
round[11].ik_sch    1651a8cd0244beda1a5da4c10640bade
round[11].ik_add    810dce0cc9db8172b3678c1e88a1b5bd
round[12].istart    ad9c7e017e55ef25bc150fe01ccb6395
round[12].is_row    adcb0f257e9c63e0bc557e951c15ef01
round[12].is_box    1859fbc28a1c00a078ed8aadc42f6109
round[12].ik_sch    a573c29fa176c498a97fce93a572c09c
round[12].ik_add    bd2a395d2b6ac438d192443e615da195
round[13].istart    84e1fd6b1a5c946fdf4938977cfbac23
round[13].is_row    84fb386f1ae1ac97df5cfd237c49946b
round[13].is_box    4f63760643e0aa85efa7213201a4e705
round[13].ik_sch    101112131415161718191a1b1c1d1e1f
round[13].ik_add    5f72641557f5bc92f7be3b291db9f91a
round[14].istart    6353e08c0960e104cd70b751bacad0e7
round[14].is_row    63cab7040953d051cd60e0e7ba70e18c
round[14].is_box    00102030405060708090a0b0c0d0e0f0
round[14].ik_sch    000102030405060708090a0b0c0d0e0f
round[14].ioutput   00112233445566778899aabbccddeeff
```

EQUIVALENT INVERSE CIPHER (DECRYPT):

```
round[ 0].iinput    8ea2b7ca516745bfeafc49904b496089
round[ 0].ik_sch    24fc79ccbf0979e9371ac23c6d68de36
round[ 1].istart    aa5ece06ee6e3c56dde68bac2621bebf
round[ 1].is_box    629deca599456db9c9f5ceaa237b5af4
round[ 1].is_row    627bceb9999d5aaac945ecf423f56da5
round[ 1].im_col    e51c9502a5c1950506a61024596b2b07
round[ 1].ik_sch    34f1d1ffbfceaa2ffce9e25f2558016e
round[ 2].istart    d1ed44fd1a0f3f2afa4ff27b7c332a69
round[ 2].is_box    5153862143fb259514920403016695e4
round[ 2].is_row    516604954353950314fb86e401922521
round[ 2].im_col    91a29306cc450d0226f4b5eaef5efed8
round[ 2].ik_sch    5e1648eb384c350a7571b746dc80e684
round[ 3].istart    cfb4dbedf4093808538502ac33de185c
round[ 3].is_box    5fc69f53ba4076bf50676aaa669c34a7
round[ 3].is_row    5f9c6abfbac634aa50409fa766677653
round[ 3].im_col    b041a94eff21ae9212278d903b8a63f6
round[ 3].ik_sch    c8a305808b3f7bd043274870d9b1e331
round[ 4].istart    78e2acce741ed5425100c5e0e23b80c7
round[ 4].is_box    c13baaeccae9b5f6705207a03b493a31
round[ 4].is_row    c14907f6ca3b3aa070e9aa313b52b5ec
round[ 4].im_col    638357cec07de6300e30d0ec4ce2a23c
round[ 4].ik_sch    b5708e13665a7de14d3d824ca9f151c2
round[ 5].istart    d6f3d9dda6279bd1430d52a0e513f3fe
round[ 5].is_box    4a7ee5c9c53de85164f348472a827e0c
round[ 5].is_row    4a824851c57e7e47643de50c2af3e8c9
round[ 5].im_col    ca6f71058c642842a315595fdf54f685
round[ 5].ik_sch    74da7ba3439c7e50c81833a09a96ab41
round[ 6].istart    beb50aa6cff856126b0d6aff45c25dc4
round[ 6].is_box    5ad2a3c55fe1b93905f3587d68a88d88
round[ 6].is_row    5aa858395fd28d7d05e1a38868f3b9c5
round[ 6].im_col    ca46f5ea835eab0b9537b6dbb221b6c2
round[ 6].ik_sch    3ca69715d32af3f22b67ffade4ccd38e
round[ 7].istart    f6e062ff507458f9be50497656ed654c
round[ 7].is_box    d6a0ab7d6cca5e695a6ca40fb953bc5d
round[ 7].is_row    d653a4696ca0bc0f5acaab5db96c5e7d
round[ 7].im_col    2a70c8da28b806e9f319ce42be4baead
round[ 7].ik_sch    f85fc4f3374605f38b844df0528e98e1
round[ 8].istart    d22f0c291ffe031a789d83b2ecc5364c
round[ 8].is_box    7f4e814ccb0cd543c175413e8307245d
round[ 8].is_row    7f074143cb4e243ec10c815d8375d54c
round[ 8].im_col    f0073ab7404a8a1fc2cba0b80df08517
round[ 8].ik_sch    de69409aef8c64e7f84d0c5fcfab2c23
round[ 9].istart    2e6e7a2dafc6eef83a86ace7c25ba934
round[ 9].is_box    c345bdfa1bc799e1a2dcaab0a857b728
round[ 9].is_row    c357aae11b45b7b0a2c7bd28a8dc99fa
round[ 9].im_col    3225fe3686e498a32593c1872b613469
round[ 9].ik_sch    aed55816cf19c100bcc24803d90ad511
round[10].istart    9cf0a62049fd59a399518984f26be178
round[10].is_box    1c17c554a4211571f970f24f0405e0c1
round[10].is_row    1c05f271a417e04ff921c5c104701554
round[10].im_col    9d1d5c462e655205c4395b7a2eac55e2
round[10].ik_sch    15c668bd31e5247d17c168b837e6207c
round[11].istart    88db34fb1f807678d3f833c2194a759e
round[11].is_box    979f2863cb3a0fc1a9e166a88e5c3fdf
round[11].is_row    975c66c1cb9f3fa8a93a28df8ee10f63
round[11].im_col    d24bfb0e1f997633cfce86e37903fe87
round[11].ik_sch    7fd7850f61cc991673db890365c89d12
```

```
round[12].istart   ad9c7e017e55ef25bc150fe01ccb6395
round[12].is_box   181c8a098aed61c2782ffba0c45900ad
round[12].is_row   1859fbc28a1c00a078ed8aadc42f6109
round[12].im_col   aec9bda23e7fd8aff96d74525cdce4e7
round[12].ik_sch   2a2840c924234cc026244cc5202748c4
round[13].istart   84e1fd6b1a5c946fdf4938977cfbac23
round[13].is_box   4fe0210543a7e706efa476850163aa32
round[13].is_row   4f63760643e0aa85efa7213201a4e705
round[13].im_col   794cf891177bfd1ddf67a744acd9c4f6
round[13].ik_sch   1a1f181d1e1b1c191217101516131411
round[14].istart   6353e08c0960e104cd70b751bacad0e7
round[14].is_box   0050a0f04090e03080d02070c01060b0
round[14].is_row   00102030405060708090a0b0c0d0e0f0
round[14].ik_sch   000102030405060708090a0b0c0d0e0f
round[14].ioutput  00112233445566778899aabbccddeeff
```

Appendix D - References

[1] AES page available via http://www.nist.gov/CryptoToolkit.[4]

[2] Computer Security Objects Register (CSOR): http://csrc.nist.gov/csor/.

[3] J. Daemen and V. Rijmen, *AES Proposal: Rijndael*, AES Algorithm Submission, September 3, 1999, available at [1].

[4] J. Daemen and V. Rijmen, *The block cipher Rijndael*, Smart Card research and Applications, LNCS 1820, Springer-Verlag, pp. 288-296.

[5] B. Gladman's AES related home page http://fp.gladman.plus.com/cryptography_technology/.

[6] A. Lee, NIST Special Publication 800-21, *Guideline for Implementing Cryptography in the Federal Government*, National Institute of Standards and Technology, November 1999.

[7] A. Menezes, P. van Oorschot, and S. Vanstone, *Handbook of Applied Cryptography*, CRC Press, New York, 1997, p. 81-83.

[8] J. Nechvatal, et. al., *Report on the Development of the Advanced Encryption Standard (AES)*, National Institute of Standards and Technology, October 2, 2000, available at [1].

[4] A complete set of documentation from the AES development effort – including announcements, public comments, analysis papers, conference proceedings, etc. – is available from this site.

FIPS PUB 198-1

FEDERAL INFORMATION PROCESSING STANDARDS PUBLICATION

The Keyed-Hash Message Authentication Code (HMAC)

CATEGORY: COMPUTER SECURITY **SUBCATEGORY: CRYPTOGRAPHY**

Information Technology Laboratory
National Institute of Standards and Technology
Gaithersburg, MD 20899-8900

July 2008

U.S. Department of Commerce
Carlos M. Gutierrez, Secretary

National Institute of Standards and Technology
James M. Turner, Deputy Director

FOREWORD

The Federal Information Processing Standards Publication Series of the National Institute of Standards and Technology (NIST) is the official series of publications relating to Standards and Guidelines adopted and promulgated under the provisions of the Federal Information Security Management Act (FISMA) of 2002.

Comments concerning FIPS publications are welcomed and should be addressed to the Director, Information Technology Laboratory, National Institute of Standards and Technology, 100 Bureau Drive, Stop 8900, Gaithersburg, MD 20899-8900.

Cita Furlani, Director
Information Technology Laboratory

Abstract

This Standard describes a keyed-hash message authentication code (HMAC), a mechanism for message authentication using cryptographic hash functions. HMAC can be used with any iterative Approved cryptographic hash function, in combination with a shared secret key.

Keywords: computer security, cryptography, HMAC, MAC, message authentication, Federal Information Processing Standards (FIPS).

Federal Information Processing Standards Publication 198-1

July 2008

Announcing the Standard for

The Keyed-Hash Message Authentication Code (HMAC)

Federal Information Processing Standards Publications (FIPS PUBS) are issued by the National Institute of Standards and Technology (NIST) after approval by the Secretary of Commerce pursuant to Section 5131 of the Information Technology Management Reform Act of 1996 (Public Law 104-106) and the Computer Security Act of 1987 (Public Law 100-235).

1. **Name of Standard.** The Keyed-Hash Message Authentication Code (HMAC) (FIPS PUB 198-1).

2. **Category of Standard.** Computer Security Standard. **Subcategory.** Cryptography.

3. **Explanation.** This Standard specifies an algorithm for applications requiring message authentication. Message authentication is achieved via the construction of a message authentication code (MAC). MACs based on cryptographic hash functions are known as HMACs.

The purpose of a MAC is to authenticate both the source of a message and its integrity without the use of any additional mechanisms. HMACs have two functionally distinct parameters, a message input and a secret key known only to the message originator and intended receiver(s). Additional applications of keyed-hash functions include their use in challenge-response identification protocols for computing responses, which are a function of both a secret key and a challenge message.

An HMAC function is used by the message sender to produce a value (the MAC) that is formed by condensing the secret key and the message input. The MAC is typically sent to the message receiver along with the message. The receiver computes the MAC on the received message using the same key and HMAC function as were used by the sender, and compares the result computed with the received MAC. If the two values match, the message has been correctly received, and the receiver is assured that the sender is a member of the community of users that share the key.

4. **Approving Authority.** Secretary of Commerce.

5. Maintenance Agency. Department of Commerce, National Institute of Standards and Technology, Information Technology Laboratory (ITL).

6. Applicability. This Standard is applicable to all Federal departments and agencies for the protection of sensitive unclassified information that is not subject to Title 10 United States Code Section 2315 (10 USC 2315) and that is not within a national security system as defined in Title 44 United States Code Section 3502(2) (44 USC 3502(2)). The adoption and use of this Standard is available to private and commercial organizations.

7. Specifications. Federal Information Processing Standard (FIPS) 198-1, The Keyed-Hash Message Authentication Code (HMAC) (affixed).

8. Implementations. The authentication mechanism described in this Standard may be implemented in software, firmware, hardware, or any combination thereof. NIST has developed a Cryptographic Module Validation Program that will test implementations for conformance with this HMAC Standard. Information on this program is available at http://csrc.nist.gov/groups/STM/index.html.

Agencies are advised that keys used for HMAC applications should not be used for other purposes.

9. Other Approved Security Functions. HMAC implementations that comply with this Standard shall employ cryptographic algorithms, cryptographic key generation algorithms and key management techniques that have been approved for protecting Federal government sensitive information. Approved cryptographic algorithms and techniques include those that are either:

a. specified in a Federal Information Processing Standard (FIPS),
b. adopted in a FIPS or NIST Recommendation, or
c. specified in the list of Approved security functions for FIPS 140-2.

10. Export Control. Certain cryptographic devices and technical data regarding them are subject to Federal export controls. Exports of cryptographic modules implementing this Standard and technical data regarding them must comply with these Federal regulations and be licensed by the Bureau of Export Administration of the U.S. Department of Commerce. Information about export regulations is available at: http://www.bis.doc.gov/index.htm.

11. Implementation Schedule. Guidance regarding the testing and validation to FIPS 198-1 and its relationship to FIPS 140-2 can be found in IG 1.10 of the Implementation Guidance for FIPS PUB 140-2 and the Cryptographic Module Validation Program at http://csrc.nist.gov/groups/STM/cmvp/index.html.

12. Qualifications. The security afforded by the HMAC function is dependent on maintaining the secrecy of the key and the use of an appropriate Approved hash function. Therefore, users must guard against disclosure of these keys. While it is the intent of this

Standard to specify a mechanism to provide message authentication, conformance to this Standard does not assure that a particular implementation is secure. It is the responsibility of the implementer to ensure that any module containing an HMAC implementation is designed and built in a secure manner.

Similarly, the use of a product containing an implementation that conforms to this Standard does not guarantee the security of the overall system in which the product is used. The responsible authority in each agency shall assure that an overall system provides an acceptable level of security.

Since a Standard of this nature must be flexible enough to adapt to advancements and innovations in science and technology, this Standard will be reviewed every five years in order to assess its adequacy.

13. Waiver Procedure: The Federal Information Security Management Act (FISMA) does not allow for waivers to Federal Information Processing Standards (FIPS) that are made mandatory by the Secretary of Commerce.

14. Where to obtain copies. This publication is available by accessing http://csrc.nist.gov/publications/. Other computer security publications are available at the same web site.

Federal Information Processing Standards Publication 198-1

Specifications for

The Keyed-Hash Message Authentication Code

TABLE OF CONTENTS

1. INTRODUCTION

Providing a way to check the integrity of information transmitted over or stored in an unreliable medium is a prime necessity in the world of open computing and communications. Mechanisms that provide such integrity checks based on a secret key are usually called message authentication codes (MACs). Typically, message authentication codes are used between two parties that share a secret key in order to authenticate information transmitted between these parties. This Standard defines a MAC that uses a cryptographic hash function in conjunction with a secret key. This mechanism is called HMAC [HMAC]. HMAC shall use an Approved cryptographic hash function [FIPS 180-3]. HMAC uses the secret key for the calculation and verification of the MACs.

2. GLOSSARY OF TERMS AND ACRONYMS

2.1 Glossary of Terms

The following definitions are used throughout this Standard:

Approved: FIPS-approved or NIST recommended. An algorithm or technique that is either 1) specified in a FIPS or NIST Recommendation, or 2) adopted in a FIPS or NIST Recommendation and specified in either the FIPS or NIST Recommendation, or in a document referenced by the FIPS or NIST Recommendation.

Cryptographic key (key): a parameter used in conjunction with a cryptographic algorithm that determines the specific operation of that algorithm. In this Standard, the cryptographic key is used by the HMAC algorithm to produce a MAC on the data.

Hash function: a mathematical function that maps a string of arbitrary length (up to a pre-determined maximum size) to a fixed length string.

Keyed-hash message authentication code (HMAC): a message authentication code that uses a cryptographic key in conjunction with a hash function.

Message Authentication Code (MAC): a cryptographic checksum that results from passing data through a message authentication algorithm. In this Standard, the message authentication algorithm is called HMAC, while the result of applying HMAC is called the MAC.

Secret key: a cryptographic key that is uniquely associated with one or more entities. The use of the term "secret" in this context does not imply a classification level; rather the term implies the need to protect the key from disclosure or substitution.

2.2 Acronyms

The following acronyms and abbreviations are used throughout this Standard:

FIPS	Federal Information Processing Standard
FIPS PUB	FIPS Publication
HMAC	Keyed-Hash Message Authentication Code
MAC	Message Authentication Code
NIST	National Institute of Standards and Technology

2.3 HMAC Parameters and Symbols

HMAC uses the following parameters:

B	Block size (in bytes) of the input to the Approved hash function.
H	An Approved hash function.
ipad	Inner pad; the byte x'36' repeated B times.
K	Secret key shared between the originator and the intended receiver(s).
K_0	The key K after any necessary pre-processing to form a B byte key.
L	Block size (in bytes) of the output of the Approved hash function.
opad	Outer pad; the byte x'5c' repeated B times.
text	The data on which the HMAC is calculated; *text* does **not** include the padded key. The length of *text* is n bits, where $0 \leq n < 2^B - 8B$.
x 'N'	Hexadecimal notation, where each symbol in the string 'N' represents 4 binary bits.
$\|\|$	Concatenation.
$\oplus$	Exclusive-Or operation.

3. CRYPTOGRAPHIC KEYS

HMAC uses a key, K, of appropriate security strength, as discussed in NIST Special Publication (SP) 800-107 [SP 800-107], Recommendation for Applications Using Approved Hash Algorithms. When an application uses a K longer than B-bytes, then it shall first hash the K using H and then use the resultant L-byte string as the key K_0; detail can be found in Table 1 in Section 4 below.

4. HMAC SPECIFICATION

To compute a MAC over the data '*text*' using the HMAC function, the following operation is performed:

$$\boldsymbol{MAC(text) = HMAC(K, text) = H((K_0 \oplus opad) \| H((K_0 \oplus ipad) \| text))}$$

Table 1 illustrates the step by step process in the HMAC algorithm, which is depicted in Figure 1.

Table 1: The HMAC Algorithm

STEPS	STEP-BY-STEP DESCRIPTION
Step 1	If the length of $K = B$: set $K_0 = K$. Go to step 4.
Step 2	If the length of $K > B$: hash K to obtain an L byte string, then append (B-L) zeros to create a B-byte string K_0 (i.e., $K_0 = H(K) \| 00...00$). Go to step 4.
Step 3	If the length of $K < B$: append zeros to the end of K to create a B-byte string K_0 (e.g., if K is 20 bytes in length and $B = 64$, then K will be appended with 44 zero bytes x'00').
Step 4	Exclusive-Or K_0 with *ipad* to produce a B-byte string: $\boldsymbol{K_0 \oplus ipad}$.
Step 5	Append the stream of data '*text*' to the string resulting from step 4: $\boldsymbol{(K_0 \oplus ipad) \| text}$.
Step 6	Apply H to the stream generated in step 5: $\boldsymbol{H((K_0 \oplus ipad) \| text)}$.
Step 7	Exclusive-Or K_0 with *opad*: $\boldsymbol{K_0 \oplus opad}$.
Step 8	Append the result from step 6 to step 7: $\boldsymbol{(K_0 \oplus opad) \| H((K_0 \oplus ipad) \| text)}$.
Step 9	Apply H to the result from step 8: $\boldsymbol{H((K_0 \oplus opad) \| H((K_0 \oplus ipad) \| text))}$.

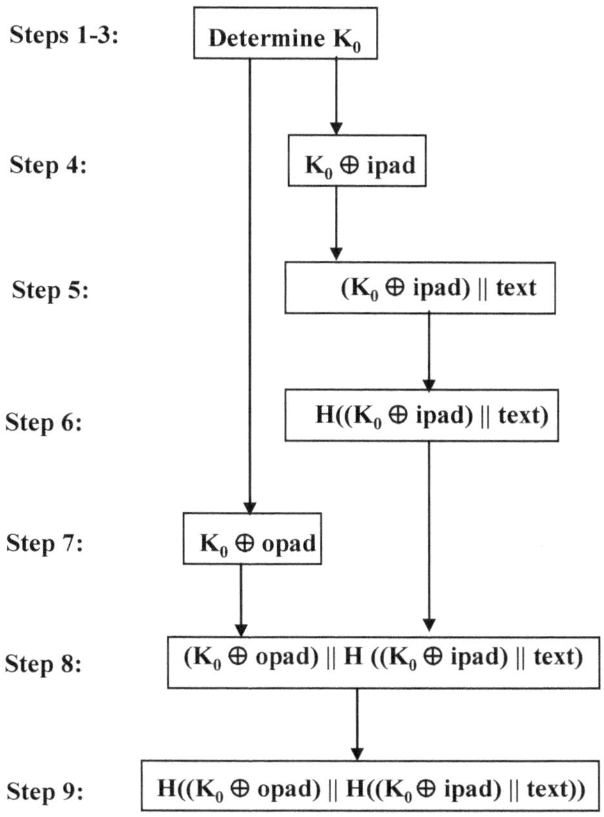

Figure 1: Illustration of the HMAC Construction

5. TRUNCATION

A well-known practice with MACs is to truncate their outputs (i.e., the length of the MACs used is less than the length of the output of the HMAC function L). Applications of this standard may truncate the outputs of the HMAC. When truncation is used, the λ leftmost bits of the output of the HMAC function shall be used as the MAC. For information about the choice of λ and the security implications of using truncated outputs of the HMAC function, see SP 800-107.

6. IMPLEMENTATION NOTE

The HMAC algorithm is specified for an arbitrary Approved iterative cryptographic hash function, H. In the HMAC algorithm, values of the *ipad* and the *opad* depend on the block size, B, of the Approved hash function. An HMAC implementation can easily replace one Approved iterative hash function, H, with another Approved iterative hash function, *H'* by generating new *ipad* and *opad* using the block size of *H'* instead of *H* as defined in Section 2.3.

Conceptually, the intermediate results of the compression function on the *B*-byte blocks ($K_0 \oplus ipad$) and ($K_0 \oplus opad$) can be precomputed once, at the time of generation of the key *K*, or before its first use. These intermediate results can be stored and then used to initialize *H* each time that a message needs to be authenticated using the same key. For each authenticated message using the key *K*, this method saves the application of the hash function of *H* on two *B*-byte blocks (i.e., on ($K \oplus ipad$) and ($K \oplus opad$)). This saving may be significant when authenticating short streams of data. **These stored intermediate values shall be treated and protected in the same manner as secret keys.**

Choosing to implement HMAC in this manner has no effect on interoperability.

Object identifiers (OIDs) for HMAC are posted at
http://csrc.nist.gov/groups/ST/crypto_apps_infra/csor/algorithms.html,
along with procedures for adding new OIDs.

Examples of HMAC are available at
http://csrc.nist.gov/groups/ST/toolkit/examples.html**.**

APPENDIX A: The Differences Between FIPS 198 and FIPS 198-1

The length of truncated HMAC outputs and their security implications in FIPS 198 is not mentioned in this Standard; instead, it is described in SP 800-107. The discussion about the limitations of MAC algorithms has been moved to SP 800-107. The examples and OIDs have been posted on the NIST web sites referenced in Section 6.

APPENDIX B: References

[HMAC] H. Krawczyk, M. Bellare, and R. Canetti, *HMAC: Keyed-Hashing for Message Authentication*, Internet Engineering Task Force, Request for Comments (RFC) 2104, February 1997.

[FIPS 180-3] National Institute of Standards and Technology, *Secure Hash Standards (SHS)*, Federal Information Processing Standards Publication 180-3, October 2008.

[SP 800-57] NIST Special Publication (SP) 800-57, *Recommendation for Key Management – Part 1: General (Revised)*, March 2007.

[SP 800-107] NIST Special Publication (SP) 800-107, *Recommendation for Applications Using Approved Hash Algorithms*, February 2009.

FIPS PUB 199

FEDERAL INFORMATION PROCESSING STANDARDS PUBLICATION

Standards for Security Categorization of Federal Information and Information Systems

---

Computer Security Division
Information Technology Laboratory
National Institute of Standards and Technology
Gaithersburg, MD 20899-8900

February 2004

U.S. DEPARTMENT OF COMMERCE
Donald L. Evans, Secretary

TECHNOLOGY ADMINISTRATION
Phillip J. Bond, Under Secretary for Technology

NATIONAL INSTITUTE OF STANDARDS AND TECHNOLOGY
Arden L. Bement, Jr., Director

FOREWORD

The Federal Information Processing Standards Publication Series of the National Institute of Standards and Technology (NIST) is the official series of publications relating to standards and guidelines adopted and promulgated under the provisions of Section 5131 of the Information Technology Management Reform Act of 1996 (Public Law 104-106) and the Federal Information Security Management Act of 2002 (Public Law 107-347). These mandates have given the Secretary of Commerce and NIST important responsibilities for improving the utilization and management of computer and related telecommunications systems in the federal government. The NIST, through its Information Technology Laboratory, provides leadership, technical guidance, and coordination of government efforts in the development of standards and guidelines in these areas.

Comments concerning Federal Information Processing Standards Publications are welcomed and should be addressed to the Director, Information Technology Laboratory, National Institute of Standards and Technology, 100 Bureau Drive, Stop 8900, Gaithersburg, MD 20899-8900.

-- SUSAN ZEVIN, ACTING DIRECTOR
INFORMATION TECHNOLOGY LABORATORY

AUTHORITY

Federal Information Processing Standards Publications (FIPS PUBS) are issued by the National Institute of Standards and Technology (NIST) after approval by the Secretary of Commerce pursuant to Section 5131 of the Information Technology Management Reform Act of 1996 (Public Law 104-106) and the Federal Information Security Management Act of 2002 (Public Law 107-347).

TABLE OF CONTENTS

1 PURPOSE

The E-Government Act of 2002 (Public Law 107-347), passed by the one hundred and seventh Congress and signed into law by the President in December 2002, recognized the importance of information security to the economic and national security interests of the United States. Title III of the E-Government Act, entitled the Federal Information Security Management Act of 2002 (FISMA), tasked NIST with responsibilities for standards and guidelines, including the development of:

- Standards to be used by all federal agencies to categorize all information and information systems collected or maintained by or on behalf of each agency based on the objectives of providing appropriate levels of information security according to a range of risk levels;
- Guidelines recommending the types of information and information systems to be included in each category; and
- Minimum information security requirements (i.e., management, operational, and technical controls), for information and information systems in each such category.

FIPS Publication 199 addresses the first task cited—to develop standards for categorizing information and information systems. Security categorization standards for information and information systems provide a common framework and understanding for expressing security that, for the federal government, promotes: (i) effective management and oversight of information security programs, including the coordination of information security efforts throughout the civilian, national security, emergency preparedness, homeland security, and law enforcement communities; and (ii) consistent reporting to the Office of Management and Budget (OMB) and Congress on the adequacy and effectiveness of information security policies, procedures, and practices. Subsequent NIST standards and guidelines will address the second and third tasks cited.

2 APPLICABILITY

These standards shall apply to: (i) all information within the federal government other than that information that has been determined pursuant to Executive Order 12958, as amended by Executive Order 13292, or any predecessor order, or by the Atomic Energy Act of 1954, as amended, to require protection against unauthorized disclosure and is marked to indicate its classified status; and (ii) all federal information systems other than those information systems designated as national security systems as defined in 44 United States Code Section 3542(b)(2). Agency officials shall use the security categorizations described in FIPS Publication 199 whenever there is a federal requirement to provide such a categorization of information or information systems. Additional security designators may be developed and used at agency discretion. State, local, and tribal governments as well as private sector organizations comprising the critical infrastructure of the United States may consider the use of these standards as appropriate. These standards are effective upon approval by the Secretary of Commerce.

3 CATEGORIZATION OF INFORMATION AND INFORMATION SYSTEMS

This publication establishes security categories for both information[1] and information systems. The security categories are based on the potential impact on an organization should certain events occur which jeopardize the information and information systems needed by the organization to accomplish its assigned mission, protect its assets, fulfill its legal responsibilities, maintain its day-to-day functions, and protect individuals. Security categories are to be used in conjunction with vulnerability and threat information in assessing the risk to an organization.

---

[1] Information is categorized according to its *information type*. An information type is a specific category of information (e.g., privacy, medical, proprietary, financial, investigative, contractor sensitive, security management) defined by an organization or, in some instances, by a specific law, Executive Order, directive, policy, or regulation.

Security Objectives

The FISMA defines three security objectives for information and information systems:

CONFIDENTIALITY

"Preserving authorized restrictions on information access and disclosure, including means for protecting personal privacy and proprietary information…" [44 U.S.C., Sec. 3542]

A loss of *confidentiality* is the unauthorized disclosure of information.

INTEGRITY

"Guarding against improper information modification or destruction, and includes ensuring information non-repudiation and authenticity…" [44 U.S.C., Sec. 3542]

A loss of *integrity* is the unauthorized modification or destruction of information.

AVAILABILITY

"Ensuring timely and reliable access to and use of information…" [44 U.S.C., SEC. 3542]

A loss of *availability* is the disruption of access to or use of information or an information system.

Potential Impact on Organizations and Individuals

FIPS Publication 199 defines three levels of *potential impact* on organizations or individuals should there be a breach of security (i.e., a loss of confidentiality, integrity, or availability). The application of these definitions must take place within the context of each organization and the overall national interest.

The *potential impact* is **LOW** if—

– The loss of confidentiality, integrity, or availability could be expected to have a **limited** adverse effect on organizational operations, organizational assets, or individuals.[2]

AMPLIFICATION: A limited adverse effect means that, for example, the loss of confidentiality, integrity, or availability might: (i) cause a degradation in mission capability to an extent and duration that the organization is able to perform its primary functions, but the effectiveness of the functions is noticeably reduced; (ii) result in minor damage to organizational assets; (iii) result in minor financial loss; or (iv) result in minor harm to individuals.

The *potential impact* is **MODERATE** if—

– The loss of confidentiality, integrity, or availability could be expected to have a **serious** adverse effect on organizational operations, organizational assets, or individuals.

AMPLIFICATION: A serious adverse effect means that, for example, the loss of confidentiality, integrity, or availability might: (i) cause a significant degradation in mission capability to an extent and duration that the organization is able to perform its primary functions, but the effectiveness of the functions is significantly reduced; (ii) result in significant damage to organizational assets; (iii) result in significant financial loss; or (iv) result in significant harm to individuals that does not involve loss of life or serious life threatening injuries.

[2] Adverse effects on individuals may include, but are not limited to, loss of the privacy to which individuals are entitled under law.

The *potential impact* is **HIGH** if—

– The loss of confidentiality, integrity, or availability could be expected to have a **severe or catastrophic** adverse effect on organizational operations, organizational assets, or individuals.

AMPLIFICATION: A severe or catastrophic adverse effect means that, for example, the loss of confidentiality, integrity, or availability might: (i) cause a severe degradation in or loss of mission capability to an extent and duration that the organization is not able to perform one or more of its primary functions; (ii) result in major damage to organizational assets; (iii) result in major financial loss; or (iv) result in severe or catastrophic harm to individuals involving loss of life or serious life threatening injuries.

Security Categorization Applied to Information Types

The security category of an information type can be associated with both user information and system information[3] and can be applicable to information in either electronic or non-electronic form. It can also be used as input in considering the appropriate security category of an information system (see description of security categories for information systems below). Establishing an appropriate security category of an information type essentially requires determining the *potential impact* for each security objective associated with the particular information type.

The generalized format for expressing the security category, SC, of an information type is:

> **SC** information type = {(**confidentiality**, *impact*), (**integrity**, *impact*), (**availability**, *impact*)},
>
> where the acceptable values for potential impact are LOW, MODERATE, HIGH, or NOT APPLICABLE.[4]

EXAMPLE 1: An organization managing *public information* on its web server determines that there is no potential impact from a loss of confidentiality (i.e., confidentiality requirements are not applicable), a moderate potential impact from a loss of integrity, and a moderate potential impact from a loss of availability. The resulting security category, SC, of this information type is expressed as:

> **SC** public information = {(**confidentiality**, NA), (**integrity**, MODERATE), (**availability**, MODERATE)}.

EXAMPLE 2: A law enforcement organization managing extremely sensitive *investigative information* determines that the potential impact from a loss of confidentiality is high, the potential impact from a loss of integrity is moderate, and the potential impact from a loss of availability is moderate. The resulting security category, SC, of this information type is expressed as:

> **SC** investigative information = {(**confidentiality**, HIGH), (**integrity**, MODERATE), (**availability**, MODERATE)}.

EXAMPLE 3: A financial organization managing routine *administrative information* (not privacy-related information) determines that the potential impact from a loss of confidentiality is low, the potential impact from a loss of integrity is low, and the potential impact from a loss of availability is low. The resulting security category, SC, of this information type is expressed as:

> **SC** administrative information = {(**confidentiality**, LOW), (**integrity**, LOW), (**availability**, LOW)}.

---

[3] System information (e.g., network routing tables, password files, and cryptographic key management information) must be protected at a level commensurate with the most critical or sensitive user information being processed, stored, or transmitted by the information system to ensure confidentiality, integrity, and availability.

[4] The potential impact value of *not applicable* only applies to the security objective of confidentiality.

Security Categorization Applied to Information Systems

Determining the security category of an information system requires slightly more analysis and must consider the security categories of all information types resident on the information system. For an information system, the potential impact values assigned to the respective security objectives (confidentiality, integrity, availability) shall be the highest values (i.e., high water mark) from among those security categories that have been determined for each type of information resident on the information system.[5]

The generalized format for expressing the security category, SC, of an information system is:

> **SC** information system = {(**confidentiality**, *impact*), (**integrity**, *impact*), (**availability**, *impact*)},
>
> where the acceptable values for potential impact are LOW, MODERATE, or HIGH.

Note that the value of *not applicable* cannot be assigned to any security objective in the context of establishing a security category for an information system. This is in recognition that there is a low minimum potential impact (i.e., low water mark) on the loss of confidentiality, integrity, and availability for an information system due to the fundamental requirement to protect the system-level processing functions and information critical to the operation of the information system.

EXAMPLE 4: An information system used for large acquisitions in a contracting organization contains both sensitive, pre-solicitation phase contract information and routine administrative information. The management within the contracting organization determines that: (i) for the sensitive contract information, the potential impact from a loss of confidentiality is moderate, the potential impact from a loss of integrity is moderate, and the potential impact from a loss of availability is low; and (ii) for the routine administrative information (non-privacy-related information), the potential impact from a loss of confidentiality is low, the potential impact from a loss of integrity is low, and the potential impact from a loss of availability is low. The resulting security categories, SC, of these information types are expressed as:

> **SC** contract information = {(**confidentiality**, MODERATE), (**integrity**, MODERATE), (**availability**, LOW)},

and

> **SC** administrative information = {(**confidentiality**, LOW), (**integrity**, LOW), (**availability**, LOW)}.

The resulting security category of the information system is expressed as:

> **SC** acquisition system = {(**confidentiality**, MODERATE), (**integrity**, MODERATE), (**availability**, LOW)},

representing the high water mark or maximum potential impact values for each security objective from the information types resident on the acquisition system.

[5] It is recognized that information systems are composed of both programs and information. Programs in execution within an information system (i.e., system processes) facilitate the processing, storage, and transmission of information and are necessary for the organization to conduct its essential mission-related functions and operations. These system processing functions also require protection and could be subject to security categorization as well. However, in the interest of simplification, it is assumed that the security categorization of all information types associated with the information system provide an appropriate *worst case* potential impact for the overall information system—thereby obviating the need to consider the system processes in the security categorization of the information system.

EXAMPLE 5: A power plant contains a SCADA (supervisory control and data acquisition) system controlling the distribution of electric power for a large military installation. The SCADA system contains both real-time sensor data and routine administrative information. The management at the power plant determines that: (i) for the sensor data being acquired by the SCADA system, there is no potential impact from a loss of confidentiality, a high potential impact from a loss of integrity, and a high potential impact from a loss of availability; and (ii) for the administrative information being processed by the system, there is a low potential impact from a loss of confidentiality, a low potential impact from a loss of integrity, and a low potential impact from a loss of availability. The resulting security categories, SC, of these information types are expressed as:

SC sensor data = {(**confidentiality**, NA), (**integrity**, HIGH), (**availability**, HIGH)},

and

SC administrative information = {(**confidentiality**, LOW), (**integrity**, LOW), (**availability**, LOW)}.

The resulting security category of the information system is initially expressed as:

SC SCADA system = {(**confidentiality**, LOW), (**integrity**, HIGH), (**availability**, HIGH)},

representing the high water mark or maximum potential impact values for each security objective from the information types resident on the SCADA system. The management at the power plant chooses to increase the potential impact from a loss of confidentiality from low to moderate reflecting a more realistic view of the potential impact on the information system should there be a security breach due to the unauthorized disclosure of system-level information or processing functions. The final security category of the information system is expressed as:

SC SCADA system = {(**confidentiality**, MODERATE), (**integrity**, HIGH), (**availability**, HIGH)}.

Table 1 summarizes the potential impact definitions for each security objective—confidentiality, integrity, and availability.

	POTENTIAL IMPACT		
Security Objective	**LOW**	**MODERATE**	**HIGH**
Confidentiality Preserving authorized restrictions on information access and disclosure, including means for protecting personal privacy and proprietary information. [44 U.S.C., SEC. 3542]	The unauthorized disclosure of information could be expected to have a **limited** adverse effect on organizational operations, organizational assets, or individuals.	The unauthorized disclosure of information could be expected to have a **serious** adverse effect on organizational operations, organizational assets, or individuals.	The unauthorized disclosure of information could be expected to have a **severe or catastrophic** adverse effect on organizational operations, organizational assets, or individuals.
Integrity Guarding against improper information modification or destruction, and includes ensuring information non-repudiation and authenticity. [44 U.S.C., SEC. 3542]	The unauthorized modification or destruction of information could be expected to have a **limited** adverse effect on organizational operations, organizational assets, or individuals.	The unauthorized modification or destruction of information could be expected to have a **serious** adverse effect on organizational operations, organizational assets, or individuals.	The unauthorized modification or destruction of information could be expected to have a **severe or catastrophic** adverse effect on organizational operations, organizational assets, or individuals.
Availability Ensuring timely and reliable access to and use of information. [44 U.S.C., SEC. 3542]	The disruption of access to or use of information or an information system could be expected to have a **limited** adverse effect on organizational operations, organizational assets, or individuals.	The disruption of access to or use of information or an information system could be expected to have a **serious** adverse effect on organizational operations, organizational assets, or individuals.	The disruption of access to or use of information or an information system could be expected to have a **severe or catastrophic** adverse effect on organizational operations, organizational assets, or individuals.

TABLE 1: POTENTIAL IMPACT DEFINITIONS FOR SECURITY OBJECTIVES

APPENDIX A TERMS AND DEFINITIONS

AVAILABILITY: Ensuring timely and reliable access to and use of information. [44 U.S.C., SEC. 3542]

CONFIDENTIALITY: Preserving authorized restrictions on information access and disclosure, including means for protecting personal privacy and proprietary information. [44 U.S.C., SEC. 3542]

EXECUTIVE AGENCY: An executive department specified in 5 U.S.C., SEC. 101; a military department specified in 5 U.S.C., SEC. 102; an independent establishment as defined in 5 U.S.C., SEC. 104(1); and a wholly owned Government corporation fully subject to the provisions of 31 U.S.C., CHAPTER 91. [41 U.S.C., SEC. 403]

FEDERAL INFORMATION SYSTEM: An information system used or operated by an executive agency, by a contractor of an executive agency, or by another organization on behalf of an executive agency. [40 U.S.C., SEC. 11331]

INFORMATION: An instance of an information type.

INFORMATION RESOURCES: Information and related resources, such as personnel, equipment, funds, and information technology. [44 U.S.C., SEC. 3502]

INFORMATION SECURITY: The protection of information and information systems from unauthorized access, use, disclosure, disruption, modification, or destruction in order to provide confidentiality, integrity, and availability. [44 U.S.C., SEC. 3542]

INFORMATION SYSTEM: A discrete set of information resources organized for the collection, processing, maintenance, use, sharing, dissemination, or disposition of information. [44 U.S.C., SEC. 3502]

INFORMATION TECHNOLOGY: Any equipment or interconnected system or subsystem of equipment that is used in the automatic acquisition, storage, manipulation, management, movement, control, display, switching, interchange, transmission, or reception of data or information by the executive agency. For purposes of the preceding sentence, equipment is used by an executive agency if the equipment is used by the executive agency directly or is used by a contractor under a contract with the executive agency which: (i) requires the use of such equipment; or (ii) requires the use, to a significant extent, of such equipment in the performance of a service or the furnishing of a product. The term information technology includes computers, ancillary equipment, software, firmware and similar procedures, services (including support services), and related resources. [40 U.S.C., SEC. 1401]

INFORMATION TYPE: A specific category of information (e.g., privacy, medical, proprietary, financial, investigative, contractor sensitive, security management), defined by an organization, or in some instances, by a specific law, Executive Order, directive, policy, or regulation.

INTEGRITY: Guarding against improper information modification or destruction, and includes ensuring information non-repudiation and authenticity. [44 U.S.C., SEC. 3542]

NATIONAL SECURITY SYSTEM: Any information system (including any telecommunications system) used or operated by an agency or by a contractor of an agency, or other organization on behalf of an agency— (i) the function, operation, or use of which involves intelligence activities; involves cryptologic activities related to national security; involves command and control of military forces; involves equipment that is an integral part of a weapon or weapons system; or is critical to the direct fulfillment of military or intelligence missions (excluding a system that is to be used for routine administrative and business applications, for example, payroll, finance, logistics, and personnel management applications); or, (ii) is protected at all times by procedures established for information that have been specifically authorized under criteria established by an Executive Order or an Act of Congress to be kept classified in the interest of national defense or foreign policy. [44 U.S.C., SEC. 3542]

SECURITY CATEGORY: The characterization of information or an information system based on an assessment of the potential impact that a loss of confidentiality, integrity, or availability of such information or information system would have on organizational operations, organizational assets, or individuals.

SECURITY CONTROLS: The management, operational, and technical controls (i.e., safeguards or countermeasures) prescribed for an information system to protect the confidentiality, integrity, and availability of the system and its information.

SECURITY OBJECTIVE: Confidentiality, integrity, or availability.

APPENDIX B REFERENCES

[1] Privacy Act of 1974 (Public Law 93-579), September 1975.

[2] Paperwork Reduction Act of 1995 (Public Law 104-13), May 1995.

[3] OMB Circular A-130, Transmittal Memorandum #4, *Management of Federal Information Resources*, November 2000.

[4] Information Technology Management Reform Act of 1996 (Public Law 104-106), August 1996.

[5] Federal Information Security Management Act of 2002 (Public Law 107-347), December 2002.

NIST SP 500-288
Specification for WS-Biometric Devices (WS-BD)

NIST SP 500-291
NIST Cloud Computing Standards Roadmap Version 2

NIST SP 500-292
NIST Cloud Computing Reference Architecture

NIST SP 500-293
US Government Cloud Computing Technology Roadmap

NIST SP 500-299
NIST Cloud Computing Security Reference Architecture

NIST SP 500-304
Data Format for the Interchange of Fingerprint, Facial & Other Biometric Information

NIST SP 800-12
An Introduction to Information Security

NIST SP 800-18
Developing Security Plans for Federal Information Systems

NIST SP 800-22
A Statistical Test Suite for Random and Pseudorandom Number Generators for Cryptographic

NIST SP 800-30
Guide for Conducting Risk Assessments

NIST SP 800-31
Intrusion Detection Systems

NIST SP 800-32
Public Key Technology and the Federal PKI Infrastructure

NIST SP 800-34
Contingency Planning Guide for Federal Information Sys

NIST SP 800-35
Guide to Information Technology Security Services

NIST SP 800-36
Guide to Selecting Information Technology Security Products

NIST SP 800-37
Applying Risk Management Framework to Federal Information

NIST SP 800-39
Managing Information Security Risk

NIST SP 800-40 R 3
Guide to Enterprise Patch Management Technologies

NIST SP 800-41
Guidelines on Firewalls and Firewall Policy

NIST SP 800-44
Guidelines on Securing Public Web Servers

NIST SP 800-45 Ver 2
Guidelines on Electronic Mail Security

NIST SP 800-46
Guide to Enterprise Telework, Remote Access, and Bring Your Own Device (BYOD) Security

NIST SP 800-47
Security Guide for Interconnecting Information Technology Systems

NIST SP 800-48
Guide to Securing Legacy IEEE 802.11 Wireless Networks

NIST SP 800-49
Federal S/MIME V3 Client Profile

NIST SP 800-53
Security and Privacy Controls for Information Systems and Organizations

NIST SP 800-53A
Assessing Security and Privacy Controls

NIST SP 800-56A
Pair-Wise Key-Establishment Schemes Using Discrete Logarithm Cryptography

NIST SP 800-57
Recommendation for Key Management

NIST SP 800-58
Security Considerations for Voice Over IP Systems

NIST SP 800-60
Guide for Mapping Types of Information and Information Systems to Security Categories

NIST SP 800-61
Computer Security Incident Handling Guide

NIST SP 800-63-3
Digital Identity Guidelines

NIST SP 800-63a
Digital Identity Guidelines - Enrollment and Identity Proofing

NIST SP 800-63b
Digital Identity Guidelines - Authentication and Lifecycle Management

NIST SP 800-63c
Digital Identity Guidelines- Federation and Assertions

NIST SP 800-64
Security Considerations in the System Development Life Cycle

NIST SP 800-66
Implementing the Health Insurance Portability and Accountability Act (HIPAA) Security Rule

NIST SP 800-67
Recommendation for the Triple Data Encryption Standard (TDEA) Block Cipher

NIST SP 800-70
National Checklist Program for IT Products

NIST SP 800-72
Guidelines on PDA Forensics

Standards List

NIST SP 800-73-4
Interfaces for Personal Identity Verification

NIST SP 800-76-2
Biometric Specifications for Personal Identity Verification

NIST SP 800-77
Guide to IPsec VPNs

NIST SP 800-79-2
Authorization of Personal Identity Verification Card Issuers (PCI) and Derived PIV Credential Issuers (DPCI)

NIST SP 800-81-2
Secure Domain Name System (DNS) Deployment Guide

NIST SP 800-82
Guide to Industrial Control Systems (ICS) Security

NIST SP 800-83
Guide to Malware Incident Prevention and Handling for Desktops and Laptops

NIST SP 800-84
Guide to Test, Training, and Exercise Programs for IT Plans and Capabilities

NIST SP 800-85A-4 PIV
Card Application and Middleware Interface Test Guidelines

NIST SP 800-85B-4 PIV
Data Model Test Guidelines (Draft)

NIST SP 800-86
Guide to Integrating Forensic Techniques into Incident Response

NIST SP 800-88
Guidelines for Media Sanitization

NIST SP 800-90A
Random Number Generation Using Deterministic Random Bit Generators

NIST SP 800-90B
Recommendation for the Entropy Sources Used for Random Bit Generation

NIST SP 800-90C
Recommendation for Random Bit Generator (RBG) Constructions - 2nd Draft

NIST SP 800-92
Guide to Computer Security Log Management

NIST SP 800-94
Guide to Intrusion Detection and Prevention Systems (IDPS)

NIST SP 800-95
Guide to Secure Web Services

NIST SP 800-97
Establishing Wireless Robust Security Networks: A Guide to IEEE 802.11i

NIST SP 800-98
Guidelines for Securing Radio Frequency Identification (RFID) Systems

NIST SP 800-101
Guidelines on Mobile Device Forensics

NIST SP 800-111
Guide to Storage Encryption Technologies for End User Devices

NIST SP 800-113
Guide to SSL VPNs

NIST SP 800-114
User's Guide to Telework and Bring Your Own Device (BYOD) Security

NIST SP 800-115
Technical Guide to Information Security Testing and Assessment

NIST SP 800-116
A Recommendation for the Use of PIV Credentials in PACS - Draft

NIST SP 800-119
Guidelines for the Secure Deployment of IPv6

NIST SP 800-120
Recommendation for EAP Methods Used in Wireless Network Access Authentication

NIST SP 800-121
Guide to Bluetooth Security

NIST SP 800-122
Guide to Protecting the Confidentiality of Personally Identifiable Information

NIST SP 800-123
Guide to General Server Security

NIST SP 800-124
Managing the Security of Mobile Devices in the Enterprise

NIST SP 800-125 & 125B
Secure Virtual Network Configuration for Virtual Machine (VM) Protection

NIST SP 800-125A
Security Recommendations for Hypervisor Deployment Draft

NIST SP 800-126
Technical Specification for the Security Content Automation Protocol (SCAP)

NIST SP 800-127
Guide to Securing WiMAX Wireless Communications

NIST SP 800-128
Guide for Security-Focused Configuration Management of Information Systems

NIST SP 800-130
A Framework for Designing Cryptographic Key Management Systems

NIST SP 800-131
Recommendation for Transitioning the Use of Cryptographic Algorithms and Key Lengths

NIST SP 800-137
Information Security Continuous Monitoring (ISCM)

NIST SP 800-142
Practical Combinatorial Testing

NIST SP 800-144
Guidelines on Security and Privacy in Public Cloud Computing

NIST SP 800-146
Cloud Computing Synopsis and Recommendations

NIST SP 800-147 & 155
BIOS Protection Guidelines & BIOS Integrity Measurement Guidelines

NIST SP 800-150
Guide to Cyber Threat Information Sharing

NIST SP 800-152
A Profile for U.S. Federal Cryptographic Key Management Systems

NIST SP 800-153
Guidelines for Securing Wireless Local Area Networks (WLANs)

NIST SP 800-154
Guide to Data-Centric System 23 Threat Modeling

NIST SP 800-155
BIOS Integrity Measurement Guidelines

NIST SP 800-156
Representation of PIV Chain-of-Trust for Import and Export

NIST SP 800-157
Guidelines for Derived Personal Identity Verification (PIV) Credentials

NIST SP 800-160
Systems Security Engineering

NIST SP 800-161
Supply Chain Risk Management Practices for Federal Information Systems and Organizations

NIST SP 800-162
Guide to Attribute Based Access Control (ABAC) Definition and Considerations

NIST SP 800-163
Vetting the Security of Mobile Applications

NIST SP 800-166
Derived PIV Application and Data Model Test Guidelines

NIST SP 800-171 R1
Protecting Controlled Unclassified Information in Nonfederal Systems

NIST SP 800-175 (A & B)
Guideline for Using Cryptographic Standards in the Federal Government

NIST SP 800-177
Trustworthy Email

NIST SP 800-178
Comparison of Attribute Based Access Control (ABAC) Standards for Data Service Applications

NIST SP 800-179
Guide to Securing Apple OS X 10.10 Systems for IT Professional

NIST SP 800-181
National Initiative for Cybersecurity Education (NICE) Cybersecurity Workforce Framework

NIST SP 800-183
Networks of 'Things'

NIST SP 800-184
Guide for Cybersecurity Event Recovery

NIST SP 800-187
Guide to LTE Security - Draft

NIST SP 800-188
De-Identifying Government Datasets - (2nd DRAFT)

NIST SP 800-190
Application Container Security Guide

NIST SP 800-191
The NIST Definition of Fog Computing

NIST SP 800-192
Verification and Test Methods for Access Control Policies/Models

NIST SP 800-193
Platform Firmware Resiliency Guidelines

NIST SP 1800-1
Securing Electronic Health Records on Mobile Devices

NIST SP 1800-2 Book 1
Identity and Access Management for Electric Utilities 1800-2a & 1800-2b

NIST SP 1800-2 Book 2
Identity and Access Management for Electric Utilities 1800-2c

NIST SP 1800-3 Book 1
Attribute Based Access Control NIST 1800-3a+b

NIST SP 1800-3 Book 2
Attribute Based Access Control NIST 1800-3c Chap 1 - 6

NIST SP 1800-3 Book 3
Attribute Based Access Control NIST1800-3c Chap 7 - 10

NIST SP 1800-4a & b
Mobile Device Security: Cloud and Hybrid Builds

NIST SP 1800-4c
Mobile Device Security: Cloud and Hybrid Builds

NIST SP 1800-5
IT Asset Management: Financial Services

NIST SP 1800-6
Domain Name Systems-Based Electronic Mail Security

NIST SP 1800-7
Situational Awareness for Electric Utilities

NIST SP 1800-8
Securing Wireless Infusion Pumps

NIST SP 1800-9
Access Rights Management for the Financial Services Sector

NIST SP 1800-11
Data Integrity Recovering from Ransomware and Other Destructive Events

NIST SP 1800-12
Derived Personal Identity Verification (PIV) Credentials

NISTIR 7298 R 2
Glossary of Key Information Security Terms

NISTIR 7497
Security Architecture Design Process for Health Information Exchanges (HIEs)

NISTIR 7628 R 1 Vol 1
Guidelines for Smart Grid Cybersecurity - Architecture, and High-Level Requirements

NISTIR 7628 R 1 Vol 2
Guidelines for Smart Grid Cybersecurity

NISTIR 7628 R 1 Vol 3
Guidelines for Smart Grid Cybersecurity - Supportive Analyses and References

NISTIR 7756
CAESARS Framework Extension: An Enterprise Continuous Monitoring Technical Refer

NISTIR 7788
Security Risk Analysis of Enterprise Networks Using Probabilistic Attack Graphs

NISTIR 7823
Advanced Metering Infrastructure Smart Meter Upgradeability Test Framework

NISTIR 7874
Guidelines for Access Control System Evaluation Metrics

NISTIR 7904
Trusted Geolocation in the Cloud: Proof of Concept Implementation

NISTIR 7924
Reference Certificate Policy

NISTIR 7987
Policy Machine: Features, Architecture, and Specification

NISTIR 8006
NIST Cloud Computing Forensic Science Challenges

NISTIR 8011 Vol 1
Automation Support for Security Control Assessments

NISTIR 8011 Vol 2
Automation Support for Security Control Assessments

NISTIR 8040
Measuring the Usability and Security of Permuted Passwords on Mobile Platforms

NISTIR 8053
De-Identification of Personal Information

NISTIR 8054
NSTIC Pilots: Catalyzing the Identity Ecosystem

NISTIR 8055
Derived Personal Identity Verification (PIV) Credentials (DPC) Proof of Concept Research

NISTIR 8060
Guidelines for the Creation of Interoperable Software Identification (SWID) Tags

NISTIR 8062
Introduction to Privacy Engineering and Risk Management in Federal Systems

NISTIR 8074 V1 & V2
Strategic U.S. Government Engagement in International Standardization to Achieve U.S. Objectives for Cybersecurity

NISTIR 8080
Usability and Security Considerations for Public Safety Mobile Authentication

NISTIR 8089
An Industrial Control System Cybersecurity Performance Testbed

NISTIR 8112
Attribute Metadata - Draft

NISTIR 8135
Identifying and Categorizing Data Types for Public Safety Mobile Applications:

NISTIR 8138
Vulnerability Description Ontology (VDO)

NISTIR 8139
Identifying Uniformity with Entropy and Divergence

NISTIR 8144
Assessing Threats to Mobile Devices & Infrastructure

NISTIR 8149
Developing Trust Frameworks to Support Identity Federations

NISTIR 8151
Dramatically Reducing Software Vulnerabilities

NISTIR 8170
The Cybersecurity Framework

NISTIR 8176
Security Assurance Requirements for Linux Application Container

Draft NISTIR 8179
Criticality Analysis Process Model

NISTIR 8183
Cybersecurity Framework Manufacturing Profile

NISTIR 8188
Key Performance Indicators for Process Control System Cybersecurity Performance Analysis

NISTIR 8192
Enhancing Resilience of the Internet and Communications Ecosystem

Whitepaper
Cybersecurity Framework Manufacturing Profile

Whitepaper
NIST Framework for Improving Critical Infrastructure Cybersecurity

Whitepaper
Challenging Security Requirements for US Government Cloud Computing Adoption

FIPS PUB 140-2
Security requirements for Cryptographic Modules

FIPS PUB 140-2 DTR
Derived Test Requirements for FIPS PUB 140-2

FIPS PUB 140-2 IG
Implementation Guidance for FIPS PUB 140-2

FIPS PUB 180-4
Secure Hash Standard (SHS)

FIPS PUB 186-4
Digital Signature Standard (DSS)

FIPS PUB 197, 198 & 199
Advanced Encryption Standard (AES), The Keyed-Hash Message Authentication Code (HMAC), Standards for Security Categorization of Federal Information and Information Systems

FIPS PUB 200
Minimum Security Requirements for Federal Information and Information Systems

FIPS PUB 201
Personal Identity Verification (PIV) of Federal Employees and Contractors

FIPS PUB 202
SHA-3 Standard: Permutation-Based Hash and Extendable-Output Functions

DFARS
Defense Federal Acquisition Regulations Supplement

FARS
Federal Acquisition Regulations

FMR
Financial Management Regulations

DHS Study
DHS Study on Mobile Device Security

OMB A-130 FISMA
OMB A-130/Federal Information Security Modernization Act

DAG
Defense Acquisition Guidebook (Chapters 1 - 10)

UFC 1-200-01
DoD Building Code (General Building Requirements)

UFC 1-200-02
High-Performance and Sustainable Building Requirements

UFC 1-201-02
Assessment of Existing Facilities for Use in Military

UFC 1-300-07A
Design Build Technical Requirements

FC 1-300-09N
Navy and Marine Corps Design Procedures

UFC 2-100-01
Installation Master Planning

UFC 3-101-01
Architecture

UFC 3-120-01
Design: Sign Standards

UFC 3-120-10
Interior Design

UFC 3-201-01
Civil Engineering

UFC 3-201-02
Landscape Architecture

UFC 3-210-10
Low Impact Development

UFC 3-230-02
Operation and Maintenance: Water Supply Systems

UFC 3-240-13fn
Industrial Water Treatment Operations and Maintenance

UFC 3-260-01
Airfield and Heliport Planning and Design

UFC 3-301-01
Structural Engineering

UFC 3-310-04
Seismic Design of Buildings

UFC 3-410-01
Heating, Ventilating, and Air Conditioning Systems

UFC 3-410-04N
Industrial Ventilation

UFC 3-420-01
Plumbing Systems

UFC 3-430-01FA
Heating and Cooling Distribution Systems

UFC 3-430-02FA
Central Steam Boiler Plants

Standards List

UFC 3-430-07
Inspection and Certification of Boilers and Unfired Pressure Vessels

UFC 3-430-08N
Central Heating Plant

UFC 3-430-09
Exterior Mechanical Utility Distribution

UFC 3-430-11
Boiler Control Systems

UFC 3-440-01
Facility-Scale Renewable Energy Systems

UFC 3-501-01
Electrical Engineering

UFC 3-520-01
Interior Electrical Systems

UFC 3-530-01
Interior and Exterior Lighting Systems and Controls

UFC 3-540-08
Utility-Scale Renewable Energy Systems

UFC 3-550-01
Exterior Electrical Power Distribution

UFC 3-550-07
Operation and Maintenance (O&M) Exterior Power Distribution Systems

UFC 3-560-01
Electrical Safety, O & M

FC 3-580-01
Telecommunications Interior Infrastructure

UC 3-600-01
Fire Protection Engineering for Facilities

UFC 3-730-01
Programming Cost Estimates for Military Construction

UFC 3-740-05
Construction Cost Estimating

UFC 3-810-01N
Navy and Marine Corps Environmental Engineering for Facility Construction

UFC 4-010-01 Chg 1
DoD Minimum Antiterrorism Standards for Buildings

UFC 4-010-06
Cybersecurity of Facility-Related Control Systems

UFC 4-020-01
DoD Security Engineering Facilities Planning Manual

UFC 4-021-02
Electronic Security Systems

UFC 4-022-01
Entry Control Facilities/Access Control Points

UFC 4-022-03
Security Fences and Gates

UFC 4-023-03
Design of Buildings to Resist Progressive Collapse

UFC 4-023-07
Design to Resist Direct Fire Weapons Effects

UFC 4-024-01
Security Engineering: Procedures for Designing Airborne Chemical, Biological, and Radiological Protection for Buildings

UFC 4-133-01
Air Traffic Control and Air Operations Facilities

FC 4-141-05N
Navy and Marine Corps Industrial Control Systems Monitoring Stations

UFC 4-440-01
Warehouses and Storage Facilities

UFC 4-510-01
Design: Military Medical Facilities

FC 4-740-02N
Navy and Marine Corps Fitness Centers

UFC 4-740-14
Design: Child Development Centers

FC 4-740-14N
Navy and Marine Corps Child Development Centers

DoD
Energy Manager's Handbook

FEMP
Operations & Maintenance Best Practices

MIL-HNDBK 1013/1a
Design Guidelines for Physical Security of Facilities

MIL-HDBK-232A
RED/BLACK Engineering-Installation Guidelines

MIL-HDBK 1195
Radio Frequency Shielded Enclosures

TM 5-601
Supervisory Control and Data Acquisition (SCADA) Systems for C4ISR Facilities

MIL-HDBK 1012/1
Electronic Facilities Engineering

ESTCP
Facility-Related Control Systems Cybersecurity Guideline

ESTCP
Facility-Related Control Systems

DoD
Self-Assessing Security Vulnerabilities & Risks of Industrial Controls

www.ingramcontent.com/pod-product-compliance
Lightning Source LLC
LaVergne TN
LVHW060146070326
832902LV00018B/2982